long distance
grandma

Janet Teitsort

long distance
grandma

staying connected
across the miles

from: Grandma
xoxo

HOWARD
PUBLISHING CO

OUR PURPOSE AT HOWARD PUBLISHING IS TO:

- *Increase faith* in the hearts of growing Christians
- *Inspire holiness* in the lives of believers
- *Instill hope* in the hearts of struggling people everywhere

BECAUSE HE'S COMING AGAIN!

Long Distance Grandma © 2005 by Janet Colsher Teitsort
All rights reserved. Printed in the United States of America
Published by Howard Publishing Co., Inc.
3117 North 7th Street, West Monroe, Louisiana 71291-2227
www.howardpublishing.com

05 06 07 08 09 10 11 12 13 14   10 9 8 7 6 5 4 3

Edited by Jennifer Stair
Interior design by John Mark Luke Designs
Cover design by Diane Whisner

Library of Congress Cataloging-in-Publication Data

Teitsort, Janet Colsher.
   Long distance grandma : how to stay connected across the miles / Janet Teitsort.
     p. cm.
   Originally published: Grand Rapids, Mich : Baker, c1998.
   ISBN 1-58229-444-5
   1. Grandparenting. 2. Grandparent and child. 3. Separation (Psychology) 4. Creative
activities and seat work. 5. Holidays. I. Title.

HQ759.9.T45 2005
306.874'5—dc22

2005046040

"The Winds" and "Rain" taken from *The Real Mother Goose,* a trademark of Scholastic, Inc. Used by permission of Scholastic of Scholastic, Inc. "Interesting Info on Easter Dates" taken from the *Holy Bible* © 1958 by the John A. Hertel Co. Quote by Audrey Sherins and Joan Holleman © 1995 by Audrey Sherins and Joan Holleman. Reprinted from *The Joy of Grandparenting* with permission from Meadowbrook Press. "Egg-cellent Scripture Sharing" taken from "The Most Egg-citing Surprise of All," copyright 1995, Focus on the Family. All rights reserved. International copyright secured. Used by permission. "Blessing in a Box" taken from *Getting Ready for College* by Polly Berent, copyright © 2003 by Polly Berent. Used by permission of Random House, Inc. Quote by Sean Desmond taken from *A Touch of the Irish* © 1995 by Sean Desmond. Used by permission of Michael O'Mara Books.

Scripture quotations not otherwise marked are taken from the *Holy Bible, New International Version®.* Copyright © 1973, 1978, 1984 by International Bible Society. Used by permission of Zondervan Publishing House. All rights reserved. Scripture quotations marked KJV are from the *King James Version.* Scripture quotations marked TLB are taken from *The Living Bible,* copyright © 1971. Used by permission of Tyndale House Publishers, Inc., Wheaton, Illinois 60189. All rights reserved. Scripture quotations marked GNB are taken from *Good News Bible/Today's English Version* © 1976, American Bible Society.

All effort has been made to locate the original source for the quotes used in this book. If you have any information that was left out of this book regarding the correct source of quotes, please contact Howard Publishing, and corrections will be made in subsequent printings.

To Jehovah-shammah
(The LORD Is There),
my husband, John,
and our family
Debbie and Gary, Dan and Karen,
Justin and Leah, Carol, Ellie, Tommy, Hannah,
James, Lainie, Sarah, and Abby

contents

january

february

march

contents

april

june

july

contents

august

september

contents

december

acknowledgments

All of us collect experiences as we go along, and sometimes we don't remember where we got our ideas. Recipes and craft ideas are passed from one friend to another like folk tales. Many have gone before me with similar ideas, and effort has been made to give credit to original sources whenever traceable.

My purpose in writing this book has been to provide grandparents with a book jam-packed with ideas for long-distance grandparenting. Many have cheered me on during the writing of this book. To the encouragers please accept my deepest gratitude. Special thanks go to:

My husband, John.

Our family—Debbie, Gary, Justin, Leah, Carol, Ellie, Tommy, Hannah, James, Lainie, Dan, Karen, Sarah, Abby, and Mom—for enriching my life. Also, to our parents and grandparents who went before us.

Susan Wales, Judy McKain, Judy Chatham, Jean Glick, Carol Layman, Terri Clark, Maxine Marsolini, Polly Berent, and Ann McCauley for their valuable input.

Rhonda Hogan and Dan Teitsort for your special expertise. I couldn't have done it without you.

To those who have supported me in prayer—my friends at Westport Baptist and the Open Door Christian Writers.

To CLASS (Christian Leaders, Authors, and Speaker Services), especially Marita Littauer for her continued support and encouragement.

And to the great people at Howard Publishing for believing in the importance of long-distance grandparenting.

dear long-distance grandma friend

Are you asking yourself, why did my children have to move? Or at least, why did they have to take the grandkids with them? You may have taken for granted that your children lived nearby. But the mobility of our society has robbed you of your grandchildren, and now you're a long-distance grandma.

You're trying not to be too dramatic about this, but you can't help but wonder how you can bake cookies and kiss skinned knees long distance. You want to listen to your grandchildren's heartaches and share their joys. You want to attend every school program and point out your grandchild to the stranger sitting next to you.

You fear your grandchildren won't even know you—or you them. But all is not lost! Remember the song that says, "Ain't no mountain high enough . . . to keep me from you"? Excuse the bad grammar, but there ain't no mountain high enough or valley low enough to keep you from having a loving and fun relationship with your grandchildren. Have love; will travel!

Love will find a way. It may be challenging to communicate your love to your grandchildren, but it will be possible. Revive the bygone art of letter writing or jump on the modern version and get e-mail. Purchase a digital camera and e-mail photos. Take it a step further and invest in a Web camera—the next best thing to being there! By all means, you'll want a camera cell phone. And the local postmaster may get to know you by name as you send packages of love to your precious little ones.

Above all, remember God is in control! Your relationship with your grandchildren will be different, but it will be OK. You can do it!

Love,

LD Grandma Janet Teitsort

ready, set, go!
points to consider

Here are some things to think about as you make your long-distance grandparenting plan:

- How often will you physically be able to visit with your grandkids? That will give you an idea of how many long-distance activities you will want to plan.

- What are the ages of your grandchildren? Younger children need to see your face and hear your voice. Older children do well with e-mail, phone calls, and letters.

- How many grandchildren do you have? How many families are involved? The number of children and families will affect the amount of packaging, mailings, time, and expense.

- What is your financial situation? Your finances will affect the types of projects and contacts you can make with your grandchildren.

- How busy are you? How much time can you devote to projects with and for your grandchildren? You should also consider your grandchildren's schedules as you plan for long-distance activities and crafts. Today's children have busy lifestyles too.

- How is your health? Will you need help with correspondence, shopping, and mailing? If so, keep projects simple.

- Take into account your personality and temperament. Are you organized or do you procrastinate? It's important to know yourself so that you can make realistic plans and experience success.

- Are you aware of the latest gadgets in technology? Some of them will make connecting with your grandkids long distance almost as good as being there. Are you willing to invest time and money into becoming a "high-tech grandma"? Come on, you can do it!

I know you're excited about beginning your long-distance grandma adventure, but let me first explain the little icons that you'll see throughout the book. Beneath the heading of each project, you'll see one or more icons. These icons let you know at a glance what kind of activities are involved in that project:

This icon indicates that a *recipe* is part of this project. Homemade goodies from Grandma's kitchen bring a touch of your love to their hearts.

Here we have a book-related activity. It might involve a trip to the library or to the bookstore (online at www.Amazon.com, www.bn.com, www.bamm.com) for the purchase of a special read-again-and-again *book*.

This is a fun one. In this speedy electronic age, we have e-mail, which zips through cyber space, and we have "snail mail," which is carried by one of our trusty postal services. This is the icon for snail mail, meaning this activity involves sending something through the *mail*.

 When separated by the miles, it's important to keep visual images of you before your grandchildren. Videotaping yourself and grandpa with a *video camera* helps you to share your life with theirs.

 E-mail is a great way to stay in touch. It's fast, it's free (except for your monthly internet provider fee), and once you get the hang of it—it's easy!

 The *Internet* puts the world at your fingertips— almost literally! You can do all kinds of research and stay up with what your grandkids are learning through this amazing connector.

 Get out the popsicle sticks, construction paper, and glitter. It's time for some creative *crafts*!

 You can use a digital *camera* or the old-fashioned film kind. If you go digital, you can send your pictures via e-mail or post them on a Web site. Either way—digital or film—take lots of pictures of your smiling faces!

OK, you are now ready to begin. Set aside a calendar to be used exclusively for grandparenting. Check the dates you want to do an activity, and then be sure to record it on the monthly legacy page when you are finished. And remember to have fun!

My Grandchildren

Name	Birth Date
1. _____	_____
2. _____	_____
3. _____	_____
4. _____	_____
5. _____	_____
6. _____	_____
7. _____	_____
8. _____	_____
9. _____	_____
10. _____	_____
11. _____	_____
12. _____	_____
13. _____	_____
14. _____	_____
15. _____	_____

Grandparents are cool to be around. They're a lot of fun.
—ELLIE RICHARDSON, AGE 15

january

January is a time of fresh beginnings. The new calendar, unblemished by forthcoming appointments, allows you to dream of doing ordinary things in a new way.

Don't despair if you are separated by miles of interstate or even an ocean. While long-distance grandparenting makes the lyric "Over the river and through the woods, to Grandmother's house we go" seem impossible, there are ways to span the miles.

Say Cheese!
Fun with Photos

No cowboy was ever faster on the draw than a grandparent
pulling a baby picture out of a wallet.
—UNKNOWN

Begin the year by taking snapshots of the outside of your home. If you live in a wintry climate, take a picture when there's snow.

- Purchase self-adhesive postcards and make a postcard of

your house or of Grandpa making a snowman. Add a few lines expressing your love for your grandkids, and they will be beaming from ear to ear!

- Send older grandkids a pack of postcards with instructions to keep you updated on their activities. As a bonus, include stamps.

- Include pictures of you and Grandpa in your daily activities so they will know what you two do when they aren't around!

- Buy a computer and a digital camera and learn to use them. E-mailing photos is easier and less expensive than developing film, once you get the hang of it. Plus, your grandkids probably know how to do it; you want them to know you can do it too! Grandmas are not so outdated, after all.

- Make calendars for each grandchild with photos of you with them, or you can e-mail electronic cards with photos attached. Don't have a computer? Many of these projects can be done at an office supply store or in the photo section of your local drugstore.

- Put together a scrapbook or photo album of the grandchildren's visit. "Talking" photo albums and frames (with your recorded message) are now available. Spend some time making a scrapbook of the time they were with you and send it to the grandkids. You both will cherish the pictures forever.

- Mail a disposable camera for each child with a note that says, "Send me a picture. I don't want to forget what you look like!"

- Purchase a photo bag (a tote bag with plastic windows on

the outside that you can slip photos into) so you can carry photos of your grandkids everywhere you go.

- Design a postage stamp or postcard with a familiar face. Go to www.Stamps.com for details.

A New Year with Lots of Cheer
Chinese New Year

Each age has deemed the new-born year the fittest time for festal cheer.
—Sir Walter Scott

Grandmothers are full of all kinds of wisdom, and this is a great time to show that to the grandkids. They've probably never heard of the Chinese New Year. (You may not have either, but shhh! They will never know.) You will get extra points for contributing to the education of your grandchildren as well as providing a fun experience.

Here's how to pull this off:

- Buy a box of fortune cookies or, better yet, a box of Scripture cookies (available at many Christian bookstores) and some chopsticks (try your local Chinese restaurant).

- Go to the library or check the Internet for some age-appropriate facts about the Chinese New Year and write them in a way that is fun and interesting for them to read. There are also several delightful children's books regarding the Chinese New Year.

- If your long-distance family has a Chinese restaurant in

their town, send them enough money for a night out. Mom and Dad will love that!

- Mail these items, and include the following recipe for your grandchildren to enjoy:

mock chow mein

- *1 pound hamburger, browned*
- *1 cup rice, prepared*
- *1 can cream of mushroom soup*
- *1 can chop-suey vegetables*
- *1 can sliced water chestnuts*
- *1 can or package chow-mein noodles*

Mix all ingredients together except noodles. Place in casserole dish. Heat in microwave or on top of stove until warm. Top with chow-mein noodles.

The Coming Attraction
Hot Chocolate and Movie Night
Drama is life with the dull parts cut out of it.
—ALFRED HITCHCOCK

Perhaps the snow has had your grandchildren cooped up all day, or perhaps they have spent a busy week at school and need a weekend treat. Either way, with the days shorter, Mom is trying to find activities to keep the kids busy when the sun goes down. You can help set the stage for a night of fun everyone will remember.

Make your own hot chocolate mix using the following recipe:

hot chocolate mix

- *1 pound Nesquik (if you like a lot of chocolate, add another ½ pound)*
- *1 pound powdered sugar*
- *1 medium container powdered creamer*
- *1 medium box dry Carnation Instant Milk*

Mix ingredients together in a big pan, using a slotted spoon to stir. Use a funnel to fill jars or put in sealable plastic bags to mail. Include directions for mixing: add three to four heaping tablespoons to a mug of hot water. The above recipe will make between five and six quarts of hot-chocolate mix.

- If you're pressed for time, buy prepared packages of hot chocolate mix and don't worry about it.

- Purchase a fun mug for each grandchild.

- Buy several packages of microwave popcorn.

- Call ahead to ask Mom what movie the grandkids would like but don't have, and purchase it.

- Check out a copy of the same movie at your local rental store.

- Mail everything to your grandkids and wait for the phone to ring. They will call to tell you how much they love their surprise!

- Find out what night they want to watch the movie, and watch it together. You can call and discuss the movie after it's over. What a fun way to connect!

Warm Up to a Good Book
January Book Selections

It is a great thing to start life with a small number of really good books which are your very own.

—SIR ARTHUR CONAN DOYLE

Curling up with a good book on a winter day is inviting for children as well as adults. Be sure to check out your library for winter books you may choose to purchase for your long-distance grandchildren.

The Mitten is a perfect January book. Several versions of this Ukrainian folk tale are in print, but a well-recognized one is by Jan Brett (Scholastic). Include some new mittens when you mail the book, if your grandchildren live in a wintry climate.

Chicken Soup with Rice by Maurice Sendak (Harper & Row) is another fun book for the beginning of the year. This rhyming book tickles the ears and is a delight to read, plus it's educational. It teaches the months of the year—perfect for January! Moms and dads will love you for contributing to the grandchildren's education. Be clever and expand on the soup idea:

- Pack some soup mugs and dry soup packets and mail with the book. Instant lunch via long-distance Grandma!

- Send the following recipe for Grandma's Chicken Soup—it's been known to shoo away wintry colds. Older granddaughters will appreciate your starting their very own collection of recipes. (Include a recipe box for these cherished recipes.)

grandma's chicken soup

- *4 boneless chicken breasts*
- *Salt and pepper to taste*
- *1 small package egg noodles*
- *4 carrots, chopped*
- *4 potatoes, diced*
- *1 small can chicken broth (optional)*
- *½ teaspoon poultry seasoning*
- *2 stalks celery, chopped*
- *1 medium onion, diced*

Pressure-cook or stew the chicken in water. While chicken is cooking, precook egg noodles in a separate pan. Remove cooked chicken, dice it, and add it back to the broth. If additional broth is needed, use canned broth. Peel, dice, and boil the potatoes, onions, and carrots. Add all ingredients (including cooked noodles) to the broth and season. Simmer for a few moments, letting the ingredients blend together. (Note: If you want the soup to go perfectly with the Chicken Soup with Rice *book, add one cup precooked rice.)*

There are numerous ways to share a book with your long-distance grandchild, no matter their age. Younger children need to see your face as they hear your voice. Older grandkids do well with just a cassette recording.

- Videotape yourself reading several wintertime books to your grandchild. Be sure to include a copy of the book when you mail the tape.
- Purchase inexpensive copies of books through school book

clubs. Check with an elementary teacher in your area or ask your school-age grandchildren to request an extra school book-club brochure from their teacher. (Their class will earn points for your order.) Suggest that your grandkids highlight books that they would like and mail the brochure to you. You select the book(s) you want to buy for them and send the order form back with a check. (Note who to write the check to; it will be on the brochure.) Using the school book club will allow you to build your grandchildren's library at a reasonable cost.

• Invest in a Web camera for all families involved, and read to your grandchildren online.

• Send cassette tapes of you reading wintertime books for your older grandchildren to listen to. (Note: be sure they have a tape player. In this day of CDs, cassette tape players are becoming obsolete.)

• Start a round-robin story with older grandkids by writing a couple of paragraphs. Mail the story to each family of grandkids, one family at a time, and let each grandchild add a couple of paragraphs to the story. Make copies of the final story and share with the family.

Hooray for the Red, White, and Blue!
Connecting with Grandchildren in the Military

Duty, Honor, Country. Those three hallowed words reverently dictate what you ought to be, what you can be, what you will be.

—GENERAL DOUGLAS MACARTHUR

14

Grandchildren in the military need lots of love and support, especially those in basic training. Since phone calls, packages, newspapers, and magazines are prohibited during the early part of this training time, here's how you can connect:

- Write daily letters about whatever you are doing that day. Even if your routine seems mundane to you, your military grandchild will be thrilled to read a line from home. The letters don't have to be long; just make them like an e-mail. (Hint: combine letters for two or three days and mail them together. Some branches of the service make recruits do fifty push-ups for each letter they receive. While the military is intent on building muscle, Grandma and Grandpa want to be kind to their grandchild. Yet most recruits will tell you they'd rather do the push-ups than not hear from home.)

- Add notes of encouragement to your letters, fortifying your military grandchild with uplifting quotes and scriptures. Grandparents, you are assuming the role of cheerleader! Cheer them to the finish!

- Check online for a Web site for the branch of the service your grandchild is in. Most branches have Web sites for military families. These sites will give you an idea of your grandchild's daily schedule and important information.

- Look for a weekly online newspaper for your grandchild's post or base. This will give you a more detailed briefing on what is happening where your grandchild is stationed. Your grandchild may be able to provide you with these Web sites.

- Do not send sugary treats like cookies and candies during basic training. Grandparents often think these will be appreciated, in spite of the "no-send" rule. But the treats will be confiscated and cause the entire group to be disciplined at a later date.

Connecting Spiritually
Sharing Prayer Requests and Devotionals
The family that prays together, stays together.
—UNKNOWN

Being away from grandchildren physically is a great opportunity to be close to them spiritually:

- Use the same devotional book, booklets, or articles as your grandchild. Then you can share spiritual insights via e-mail, phone, or in letters.

- Ask your grandkids to send their prayer requests by e-mail or phone. Keep a log of answered prayers and suggest your grandkids do likewise. Our faith grows as we see God at work in our lives!

Grand Tip of the Month
Make the New Year "Grand" as You Grandparent Long Distance!
Nobody can do for little children what grandparents do. Grandparents sort of sprinkle stardust over the lives of little children.
—ALEX HALEY

Sing a lullaby to your infant or toddler grandchild over the phone. You don't have to be a professional singer to share a tune with your little ones. You're already special; you're the grandparent! Camera cell phones can be used to show your little ones a picture of Grandma and Grandpa. If Mom and Dad don't have a camera phone, suggest that they hold a photograph of you as you sing.

Recording the Legacy

Date_____

Long-distance activity/project _____

_____

Here's what my grandkids said_____

_____

Date_____

Long-distance activity/project _____

_____

Here's what my grandkids said_____

_____

Date_____

Long-distance activity/project _____

_____

Here's what my grandkids said_____

_____

Notes

_____

_____

_____

_____

_____

_____

_____

_____

Grandma's eyes sparkled with love when she looked at me.
—LD GRANDMA JANET TEITSORT

february

February may be the shortest month of the year, but it's filled with fun holidays! You will have lots of opportunities to try out your long-distance grandparenting skills this month. Whether you decide to keep it simple or celebrate with a lot of fanfare, you're bound to win the hearts of your grandkids.

Warm a Grandchild's Heart
Valentine's Day

Grandparents have fun ideas.
—JAMES RICHARDSON, AGE 6

There are lots of ways to share long-distance hugs and kisses with your grandchildren. Mail packages of love by sending surprises and sweet treats.

- Send younger grandkids a new box of crayons and a coloring book in which you've colored a picture.

- Touch the hearts of the younger grandkids by mailing

them a box of candy hearts with cute sayings. These treats are relatively inexpensive, but little ones love them!

- Send older grandkids a phone card so they can call you anytime they want to.

- Mail older grandkids the scented perfume/cologne samplers that are often tucked in magazines and department-store brochures. These samples tell the teens that you're thinking of them, plus it allows them to try the newest fragrances.

- Mail your grandkids a batch of sugar cookies. Pack the cookies in a box by layering them between sheets of paper towels to prevent breakage. Have problems with cookie cutters and cookie dough? Then just send a batch of Snickerdoodles.

snickerdoodles

- *2 sticks margarine*
- *¾ teaspoon baking soda*
- *1½ cups sugar, separated*
- *pinch of salt*
- *2 eggs*
- *2¾ cups flour*
- *2 teaspoons cream of tartar*
- *1 tablespoon ground cinnamon*

Mix 1 tablespoon cinnamon and 1 cup sugar in a separate bowl. Blend margarine, ½ cup sugar, and eggs. Add cream of tartar, baking soda, salt, and flour to blended mixture and mix thoroughly. Form dough into balls the size of small walnuts. Roll dough balls in mixture of cinnamon and sugar or colored sugar. Bake eight to ten minutes on an ungreased cookie sheet at 400 degrees. Don't be alarmed to see the centers of the Snickerdoodles rise then fall during baking. This is what they are supposed to do. This recipe yields four to five dozen cookies.

- If you are short on time, mail a box of graham crackers, canned frosting, and candy sprinkles or red candy hearts. The busiest grandparent can manage this, and it's still a loving way to send cookies. That's what counts! Include some plastic knives and valentine napkins in your mailing. The little ones will be thrilled to get to decorate their own valentine treats.

- Send a box of paper doilies, red construction paper or wrapping paper, glue sticks, children's scissors, and tape for your little creative geniuses. Challenge your grandkids to design an old-fashioned valentine box. Be sure to make a sample and take a picture to mail so they will get the idea. You could even videotape yourself making one. Tell them about boxes you made as a kid and explain what you are doing as you fashion a valentine box. They will love watching the tape.

- Decorate a valentine sweatshirt for your grandchild. This project is a snap with the preprinted fabric and adhesive bonding available today. Just tell the clerk at your fabric store what you want to do. Ordinary sweatshirts become something special when Grandma adds her creative touch. (Hint: after age five or six, your grandchildren will appreciate a gift card to a clothing store. Decorated sweatshirts are not popular after a certain age. Use this idea when your grandchildren are toddlers or in early elementary school.)

Mold Their Hearts
Projects for Preteens and Teens

Yet, O LORD, you are our Father. We are the clay, you
are the potter; we are all the work of your hand.

—ISAIAH 64:8

We must not forget that older grandchildren like special attention too. When doing the following projects long distance, videotape yourself demonstrating the crafty endeavor and then mail the tape along with the supplies and samples to them.

love's sweet scent
perfumed wax hearts

One project that is challenging and definitely for older grandkids is making scented wax hearts. They are inexpensive, quickly made, and are nice gifts for friends and teachers. These are fun to make and smell good too!

You will need:

- *2 scented votive candles*
- *Heart-shaped clay cookie mold*
- *Electric potpourri pot or a tin can placed in a saucepan of water*
- *Small amount of narrow ribbon*
- *Nail or other sharp object to form a hole in the wax*

Do:

1. *Melt candles in a potpourri pot. If you are using a tin can, place the candles inside the can and place the can in a saucepan of water.*

2. *Heat on low until the candle wax is melted. Discard the wicks.*

3. *Pour the melted wax into the mold.*

4. *Let the wax cool almost to room temperature, then punch a hole at the top of the heart to thread the ribbon through.*

5. *Finish cooling the mold to room temperature.*

6. *Place the mold in the freezer for a minute or two. Let it get thoroughly cold, but not frozen.*

7. *Remove cookie mold from freezer and turn it upside down. The newly formed wax heart will pop right out.*

8. *Thread enough ribbon through the hole so that it makes a large loop for hanging.*

9. *Attach a verse such as Ephesians 5:2: "Be full of love for others, following the example of Christ who loved you and gave himself to God as a sacrifice to take away your sins. And God was pleased, for Christ's love for you was like sweet perfume to him" (TLB).*

how sweet it is!
heart-shaped suckers

- *Heart-shaped tin cookie mold (each tin makes a dozen hearts)*
- *Sucker sticks*

- *Small cellophane bags for wrapping suckers*
- *Curling ribbon*
- *Bags of LifeSavers brand Creme Savers*
- *Nonstick cooking spray*

Spray the heart-shaped cookie molds with nonstick cooking spray (wipe excess with a paper towel). Place twelve candies in each mold, stacking them on top of each other. Bake at 265 degrees for fourteen minutes.

Place sucker sticks in molds and let cool to room temperature, then pop the heart-shaped candy out of the molds. Slip the candies into a cellophane bag and tie shut with curling ribbon. Don't forget to mail the ones you make along with your videotape!

Connecting Spiritually
Collecting Bible Verses

Thy word is a lamp unto my feet, and a light unto my path.
—PSALM 119:105 KJV

Since February is all about touching hearts, try this unique way of spiritual sharing:

- Send a round-robin letter or e-mail among family members asking them to share their favorite Bible verse or inspirational quote. Be sure to ask them to express why a particular verse or quote is special to them. Share the list with all participating family members.

- Grandmas can tuck these special verses and quotes in their Bible or prayer journals and refer back to them. They are great pick-me-ups when the miles seem too long. The list of favorites can be added to through the years.

Mixing Up a Batch of Grandkids
Blended Families

Love multiplies when you are blessed to be a grandparent not only to your biological grandchildren, but also to blended-in grand children. Do away with the tags of *step* and *blended* grandkids. If you have to have a tag— sometimes in conversation, you may need to explain that you have a blended family—refer to them as *bonus* grandchildren. As a loving grandparent of a mixed batch of grandkids, you'll discover that your love is multiplied. Here are some loving things to do for your *mixed batch* of grandkids:

- Include bonus and biological grandkids' names on videotapes, letters, or packages that you mail.

- E-mail or phone bonus grandkids like you do your natural-born grandchildren.

- Spend the same amount on gifts. Don't get technical to the penny—don't do that on your biological grandkids either. It's a known fact that older kids' clothes and gifts cost more than toddlers'. Just be sure they are similar types of gifts.

- Never use (in front of grandkids) the term *step* or *biological* or any tag that isolates one grandchild from another. When introducing a mixed batch of grandkids, do not differentiate. Simply say, "There are my grandchildren."

- Invite bonus grandchildren to come for a visit as often as you invite your other grandkids. If having all the grandkids come and stay at the same time is too much, you might try inviting one bonus grandchild with one biological grandchild (if they get along with each other).

- Display photos of the entire mixed batch—bonus and biological grandkids. Also, hang all the grandkids' artistic drawings on the refrigerator—not just the drawings from biological artists.

- Cooperate fully with the bonus grandkids' original family.

Short on Days; Long on Holidays
Celebrating February's Special Days

February is merely as long as is needed to pass the time until March.
—DR. J. R. STOCKTON

February is our shortest month, but it's not short on celebrations! In addition to Valentine's Day, Groundhog Day and Presidents' Day also fall within this month. Many books on the market relate stories about these holidays, and you can take advantage of the opportunity to celebrate these holidays with your children. Here are a few ideas:

Groundhog Day

- Check out where the folklore of Groundhog Day originated. There's lots of information on the Internet and at the library. Your grandkids can learn about the legend and also scientific facts about the groundhog, sundials, and shadows. It will be a learning experience for all of you.

- Share extended weather forecasts for yours and your grandchild's city. Start this project about a week before Groundhog Day. Forecasts can be easily obtained via the Internet or in the newspaper. Just for fun, predict whether the groundhog will see his shadow.

Presidents' Day

- Make a cassette or videotape with Grandpa and Grandma each reading a story about our famous presidents. Mail the tape along with a copy of the book. Be sure to include some books for the older grandkids to read.

- Use a Web camera and read books about Washington and Lincoln to your grandchild online. That way you can interact with each other as you read.

- Go to a hobby or party shop and purchase toothpick-sized American flags. Purchase a box of cellophane-wrapped cupcakes. Write a note for Mom to add the flags to the cakes before serving. Mail all these along with a book about Washington and Lincoln. They'll enjoy celebrating Presidents' Day with this patriotic treat.

- Trade historical facts about these two presidents with school-age grandchildren. Challenge them to send you five facts about Lincoln's or Washington's life. Give them bonus points if they are little-known facts. Using the Internet and e-mail is ideal for this project, but you can also send the facts by "snail mail" (regular postal service).

Heartwarming Books
February Book Selections

Another way you can celebrate February's special days with your grandchildren is by sending them one of the many wonderful books about these holidays. Don't forget to videotape or record an audiotape of you reading the book when you mail it to your grandkids!

Here are two delightful books that will enlighten young readers about America's famous presidents with February birthdays:

George Washington: A Picture Book Biography (Blue Ribbon Book) by James Giblin and illustrated by Michael Dooling (Scholastic) has beautiful pictures and an informative text. The storyline highlights the key points about America's first president.

Abe Lincoln: The Boy Who Loved Books by Kay Winters and illustrated by Nancy Carpenter (Simon and Schuster Children's Publishing) is a must-read in the introduction of famous American presidents.

For Groundhog Day and Valentine's Day, try these two books from the Fluffy Series, about a classroom guinea pig:

Fluffy Meets the Groundhog (Hello Reader Level 3) by Kate McMullan and illustrated by Mavis Smith (Cartwheel Books, Scholastic Imprint). This is an informative and funny story about a classroom guinea pig that meets the groundhog. Level 3 readers are for beginners who are graduating from reading simple sentences to paragraphs. But younger children would love to have Grandma and Grandpa read this inexpensive but fun series to them.

Fluffy's Valentine's Day (Hello Reader Level 3) by Kate McMullan and illustrated by Mavis Smith (Cartwheel Books, Scholastic Imprint) is a perfect book for this holiday. The children in the story are to make valentine boxes. This is a perfect spin-off for Grandma and Grandpa to share about a valentine box they made as a child.

And the Beat Goes On
Leaving a Legacy

What a wonderful contribution our grandmothers and grandfathers can make if they will share some of the rich experiences and their testimonies with their children and grandchildren.
—VAUGHN J. FEATHERSTONE

Before I leave this section on February, I want to make a suggestion. I think you will definitely want to invest in a Web camera, but there is an advantage to making videotapes too. If you make a monthly keepsake video of you reading or talking to your grandchildren, what a unique legacy they will acquire over the years. Get Grandpa involved too!

Just think, many years from now, your grandchild might be saying, "This was my grandpa and grandma." You could even include Bible stories. What a heritage!

Grand Tip of the Month
Bridge the Miles as You Touch Hearts

Surely, two of the most satisfying experiences in life must be those of being a grandchild or a grandparent.
—DONALD A. NORBERG

Include *bonus* grandchildren on your grandma necklace and bracelet.

Recording the Legacy

Date_____

Long-distance activity/project _____

_____

Here's what my grandkids said_____

_____

Date_____

Long-distance activity/project _____

_____

Here's what my grandkids said_____

_____

Date_____

Long-distance activity/project _____

_____

Here's what my grandkids said_____

_____

Notes

_____

_____

_____

_____

_____

_____

_____

march

Blustery or gentle, March winds carry the promise of spring. Our spirits are lifted upward like Mary Poppins with her umbrella. The gray and brown shades of winter give way to the variegated spring greens. We are filled with new energy and hope.

Hope is a strong word that rings with promise. We hope for meaningful relationships with our grandchildren. We feel a renewed motivation to make the effort to bridge the miles.

Irish Eyes Are Smiling
St. Patrick's Day and Irish History

People will not look forward to posterity who never look backward to their ancestors.

—EDMUND BURKE

The Irish know about hope. Hope for a better life caused many of them to immigrate to America. St. Patrick's Day falls during March, making this the ideal month to share genealogy about your Irish ancestry with the younger generation. No Irish relatives? You

33

can still have fun learning about the steadfastness of the Irish people. Here are some ideas to get you started:

- Visit the library or use your home computer to view a map of Ireland. If you had Irish ancestors, pinpoint where they lived and note when they arrived in America.

- Do a study of Ellis Island and what it was like for incoming immigrants. The depth of your study will depend on the age of your grandchildren.

- Research on the Internet (with school-age grandchildren) about the potato famine that occurred in Ireland. Discover how it affected the Irish.

- Make a cassette tape telling about the hearty potato and the Irish famine to your younger grandchildren. Then mail the grandkids some washable paints and art paper. Include a note asking Mom to slice potatoes in half and let them make potato prints. Just dip the potato halves in paint and print away on the paper. Be sure to ask the grandkids to mail you a print for your refrigerator door.

- Explain to your grandkids how potatoes grow. (If you didn't grow up with a garden, you may have to do a little research.) Explain that those little, white squiggly things growing out of the potato are buds and are called eyes. If you have ever raised potatoes in a garden or harvested them, be sure to relate how they are planted and harvested.

- Share your favorite potato dishes, such as French fries or potato soup. See how many different ways you can think of to fix the popular potato.

- Send them the following recipe for Grandma's Potato Stew:

grandma's potato stew

- *1 pound cubed beef*
- *Salt and pepper*
- *Potatoes*
- *Carrots, onions, and celery (can use a bag of frozen vegetables)*
- *2 cups water*

Place the stew meat in the bottom of the Crock-Pot. Sprinkle with salt and pepper. Add diced vegetables (including potatoes), then water. The Crock-Pot should be about half full. Cook on low for approximately ten to twelve hours. Tasty!

- Share Irish blessings and proverbs with older grandchildren. Your Irish family may have been passing them down through the years. If not, share this traditional Irish blessing:

> *May the road rise to meet you.*
> *May the wind be always at your back.*
> *May the sun shine warm upon your face,*
> *The rains fall soft upon your fields.*
> *And until we meet again,*
> *May God hold you in the hollow of his hand.*

Dancing in the Wind
Weather Watching

Sunshine is delicious, rain is refreshing, wind braces us up, snow is exhilarating; there is really no such thing as bad weather, only different kinds of good weather.

—JOHN RUSKIN

March is an opportune time to correspond with your grandchildren about the weather. Tune in to the Weather Channel on TV or use the Internet or your local newspaper to gather weather facts. As you explore simple meteorology with your grandkids, get Mom and Dad involved. They'll be happy to help; this is an educational, as well as a grandparent sharing experience. School-age grandchildren may even be able to get extra credit for their weather research if they show the teacher their findings.

Here are some great ways for you and your grandkids to become weather-wise:

- Clip the weather charts from your daily paper and mail them to your grandkids. Have them compare your charts with the ones in their hometown paper.

- Mail your grandchildren some books on weather. After you've made your selection for the younger grandchildren, send a cassette or videotape of you reading them. Get Grandpa involved too—take turns reading books. Don't forget the possibility of using a Web camera. These are worth the investment and the next best thing to being there! Send e-mails or letters back and forth discussing the water cycle, rainbows, and cloud formations.

- Send a pocket notebook to younger children and suggest they play weatherperson. Each day have them draw a picture of their local weather. After a week of recording, they can tear out the sheets and mail them to you. Be sure to include a self-addressed stamped envelope. (Tip: Stamps and envelopes are always nice to include if you want replies. Mom and Dad don't always have time to run out and buy these.)

- Read Charles Shaw's *It Looked Like Spilt Milk* (Harper) to younger grandkids. Along with the book, mail some white chalk and blue construction paper for cloud-making pictures. Suggest that the grandchildren take Mom and Dad outside to do some cloud watching. Be sure to ask them to mail you a picture for your refrigerator.

• Include a note to Mom and Dad in your package, asking them to purchase some saltine crackers and a bag of marshmallows. (If you try to mail saltine crackers and marshmallows, they might arrive in a crumbly, sticky mess, resembling anything but a cloud.) These ingredients are the makings for Marshmallow Clouds —yummy treats that delight all ages. Try one!

marshmallow clouds

• *Large marshmallows*
• *Saltine crackers*

Place individual saltine crackers in a glass baking dish and put a marshmallow on each saltine square. Place the dish in the microwave for ten to twenty seconds (microwaves differ in heating time—watch for them to puff up, then shut off). The marshmallows will puff up like clouds. Be careful! Let them cool. They're delicious!

• Use the Internet or library and learn how different types of clouds are formed. Discuss this info with your grandkids.

• Research online with older grandkids how tornados and hurricanes are formed (with Mom or Dad's permission, of course). Contrast the two and explain which is common to your individual states. Discuss an emergency plan for your grandkids' home and your home in the event of a tornado or hurricane.

Blowing in the Wind
Tossing Around More Ideas

East gave a feast;
North laid the cloth;
West did his best;
South burnt his mouth
Eating cold potato.

—"The Winds"

If your grandchildren live in a wintry climate, they are thrilled to get outside as March promises spring. Wind up windy-day activities by doing one or more of the following:

- Treat your grandkids to books on paper-airplane flying. Be sure to tuck in some inexpensive balsa-wood airplane flyers. They were fun when we were young, and they're still fun!

- Mail a "March winds" store gift certificate for each grandchild so they can go shopping with Mom or Dad and buy a kite or pinwheel. Fun, fun, fun! (Tip: most stores use plastic gift cards. Younger grandkids think they have a charge card and feel so important!)

- Pack and mail a shoebox full of craft supplies to make a pinwheel or windsock. Include child-safe scissors, crepe-paper streamers, glue sticks, tape, paper fasteners or brads (purchase at craft or office supply store), and construction paper. You can even demonstrate how to do the following projects on videotape or Web camera:

how to make a pinwheel

You will need:

- *8½ x 11-inch sheet of paper*
- *Ruler*
- *Paper fastener or brad*
- *Drinking straw*
- *Scissors*

Do:

1. *Measure and cut an 8½ x 11-inch sheet of paper to form an 8½-inch square.*

2. *Lay a ruler diagonally across the square. Mark a 5½-inch line in from each corner.*

3. *Cut on each line and fold every other flap to the center.*

4. *Insert a paper fastener, or brad, through the center to secure the flaps.*

5. *Make vertical slits near one end of a drinking straw. (Mom and Dad will need to make the slits with scissors, or grandparents can slit the drinking straw before mailing.) Push the ends of the brad through the slits, then open the ends of the brad.*

how to make a windsock

You will need:

- *Construction paper*
- *Glue (or stapler)*

- *Twelve-inch crepe-paper streamers*
- *Hole punch*
- *Twelve-inch piece of string or yarn*

Do:

1. *Use a sheet of construction paper to form a cylinder, and glue or staple it.*

2. *Attach twelve-inch crepe-paper streamers, approximately two inches apart around one end of the cylinder. This will be the bottom of the windsock.*

3. *Punch two holes directly across from each other at the top of the cylinder.*

4. *Thread a twelve-inch piece of string or yarn through the holes for hanging.*

Escaping the Wind
Windy-Day Books

Reading is a basic tool in the living of a good life.
—Joseph Addison

Escape the wind and snuggle inside with a windy-day book. Help your grandkids celebrate March with these fun books. Don't forget to check online bookstores, your library, and local bookstores for new releases.

Gusts and Gales by Josepha Sherman, illustrated by Omarr Wesley (Picture Window Books), is about the different types of wind. Plus—it gives directions for making a tornado in a bottle!

Like a Windy Day by Frank Asch and Devin Asch (Gulliver Books) is a good one for your toddler grandchildren. This rhyming book has fun illustrations!

Arty Facts: Weather and Art Activities by Janet Sacks (Crabtree Publishing) is a must-have. This book covers numerous weather terms and connects them with clever art projects. You'll have great fun sending your grandchildren the supplies to make a hibernation box or a mining greenhouse—fun, fun, fun!

Winnie the Pooh and the Blustery Day by Teddy Slater, illustrated by Bill Langley and Diana Wakeman (Disney Press), is a timeless book children love. Join Pooh on Windsday.

Green Eggs and Ham
Happy Birthday, Dr. Seuss!

*Green is the prime color of the world, and
that from which its loveliness arises.*
—PEDRO CALDERON DE LA BARCHA

Since March is a time to celebrate all things green, celebrate Dr. Seuss's birthday (March 2) with the following green-themed activities based on his classic book *Green Eggs and Ham* (Random House):

- Set up the camcorder and videotape yourself reading the book to your grandkids, then stir up a batch of green eggs and ham for Grandpa's breakfast. Maybe you can enlist Mom and Dad in fixing this unusual breakfast for your grandkids.

- Read several Dr. Seuss books on the videotape. Your grandkids will love them! Be sure to send some birthday hats (can be purchased at party supply stores) with your package to celebrate Dr. Seuss's birthday on March 2. The younger grandkids will love wearing the party hats as Grandpa and Grandma read to them.

- Check online, then send Mom and Dad a few Web sites that feature Dr. Seuss games, celebrations, and activities.

- Mail a Dr. Seuss video—fun for all!

With a Roar and a Baa
Celebrating Spring's Arrival

And forget not that the earth delights to feel your bare feet and the winds long to play with your hair . . .
—KAHLIL GIBRAN

The earth awakens from a long winter's sleep. You can sense God's heartbeat in nature as the season bursts forth. Every year it seems like the grass turns green and flowers sprout in the blink of an eye. As spring flowers poke up their heads to say hello, challenge your grandchildren to become observers of nature with some of the following activities:

- Suggest that the grandkids adopt a tree, a clump of flowers, or a patch of grass for a spring watch. Grandpa and Grandma, you need to choose an area at your home to observe too.

- Mail a one-time-use outdoor camera for this project. Have the grandkids snap a picture of their selected area every day for a period of three weeks. Grandparents, do the same with your area. Supply funds to pay for the film's processing. Younger grandchildren are thrilled to have their own out-door-use camera. Be sure to mail a small photo album to store these photos. Enlist Mom or Dad to write down the grandkids' comments on nature changes.

- Check with Mom and Dad first and get their permission for the kids to use their digital camera. Then handle this project with school-age grandchildren via the Internet. E-mail the pictures back and forth, noting the changes of nature.

- Snap a spring photo of the outside of your home. Buy pre-cut adhesive postcards at a camera store or drugstore photo department. Then mount your photo to the sticky side of the card and presto! You have a spring postcard of Grandma and Grandpa's house. Maybe you can get a neighbor to snap the photo so you both can be in the picture. Send these postcards for each season.

Connecting Spiritually
The Irish Shamrock and the Trinity

Therefore go and make disciples of all nations, baptizing them in the name of the Father and of the Son and of the Holy Spirit.
—MATTHEW 28:19

Use the Irish shamrock to teach about the Triune (three-in-one) God: the Father, the Son, and the Holy Spirit. Let each leaf represent one person of the Trinity. Point out how all three leaves make up one shamrock, just as the three Persons of the Trinity make up one God, who supplies all our needs.

How Fast the Years Go By
Grandkids at College
Your education is your life—guard it well.
—PROVERBS 4:13 GNB

You were the beaming grandparents at last spring's high-school graduation. How proudly you pointed out your "grand-grad." Now almost a year has passed, and your college grand is approaching finals. Here are some tips on how you can help:

- Pray for them to be disciplined in their study habits.

- Pray for their minds to be keen and alert, soaking up knowledge for test finals.

- Send encouraging e-mails and cards via the postal service.

- Mail care packages filled with nutritional treats such as nuts, granola bars, and cheese crackers.

- Let them know you are cheering them on every step of the way!

Grand Tip of the Month
March On in Your Endeavor to Grandparent Long Distance!
*Grandmothers are the people who take delight
in hearing babies breathing on the telephone.*
—UNKNOWN

List one grandchild's name per day or per week (depending on how many grandchildren you have) on your Palm Pilot or daily planner. Then connect with that grandchild one-on-one via e-mail, phone, or letter. When you've gone through the entire list, start

over. And don't forget to connect with your adult children! They
need attention too!

Recording the Legacy

Date_____

Long-distance activity/project _____

_____

Here's what my grandkids said_____

_____

Date_____

Long-distance activity/project _____

_____

Here's what my grandkids said_____

_____

Date_____

Long-distance activity/project _____

_____

Here's what my grandkids said_____

_____

Notes

_____

_____

_____

_____

_____

april

Brooks are babbling, blossoms are blooming, and buds are becoming full-sized leaves. All the earth is echoing the theme of new life. The drama of rebirth continues to unfold in flower beds throughout the land and on farms in the rural countryside. Your family may even be excitedly awaiting the birth of new pets. What a wonderful time to celebrate the resurrection of our Savior and the new life that Christ enables us to have!

When Is Easter?
Interesting Info on Easter Dates

Do you ever wonder why Easter falls on a different day each year? Here are a few interesting facts about Easter dates that you can share with your grandchildren:

- Easter sometimes falls in March and sometimes in April.

- The First Council of Nicaea (AD 325) settled the dispute as to when Easter would occur.

- The Council of Nicaea declared the celebration would take place on the first Sunday after the March 21 full moon. If the full moon occurs on a Sunday, Easter is set for the next Sunday.

- The Easter celebration never occurs before March 22 or after April 25.

- Easter is a celebration commemorating the resurrection of our Lord and Savior, Jesus Christ.

- The celebration's name in Greek, French, and other Roman languages is taken from the Hebrew *Pesach,* meaning Passover.

- The English name comes from the Anglo-Saxon *Eostre,* an April festival celebrating the goddess of light, or spring.

- The custom of wearing new clothes on Easter originated as a symbol of our new life in Christ.

Connecting Spiritually

Hands-On Easter Teaching Activities

Yet a little while, and the world seeth me no more;
but ye see me: because I live, ye shall live also.
—JOHN 14:19 KJV

Egg-cellent Scripture Sharing

You can use Easter eggs to teach your grandchildren the biblical message of Easter. Purchase a dozen plastic eggs and number the outside of the eggs from 1 to 12. Write the twelve Scripture references (below) on small pieces of paper. Fill each egg with the corresponding verse and small object listed:

1. Cotton ball sprayed with perfume (Matthew 26:6–13)

2. Dime (Matthew 26:14–16)

3. Bread crust (Matthew 26:17–19)

4. Olive in plastic wrap (Matthew 26:30, 36–46)

5. Piece of paper with a lipstick kiss on it (Matthew 26:47–68)

6. Small, dried chicken bone (Matthew 26:31–35, 69–75)

7. Piece of string or yarn and a clod of dirt (Matthew 27:1–10)

8. Piece of red cloth (Matthew 27:11–31)

9. Two twigs tied with dental floss to form the shape of a cross, and two nails (Matthew 27:32–44)

10. Piece of a sponge (Matthew 27:45–56)

11. Rock or marble (Matthew 27:57–65)

12. Nothing (Matthew 28:1–8)

Have your grandchildren place the eggs in a carton on their dining-room table or wherever their family gets together. Twelve days before Easter, they should open the first egg, read the Scripture passage, and discuss the egg's relevance to the Easter story. Tell them to open one egg a day in order through Easter Sunday. Hearts will open with the newness of life these eggs will foster.

If you are pressed for time, Family Life Publishing has come out with a book and set of filled plastic eggs called *Resurrection Eggs* (© 2002). Whichever way you choose, the importance is sharing the Resurrection story with your grand family.

the angel rolled the stone away: resurrection rolls

If you will be visiting your grandchildren for Easter, this is a great activity to do together. It's a delicious way to celebrate the Resurrection!

- *1 tube crescent rolls*
- *Melted margarine*
- *Large marshmallows*
- *Cinnamon*
- *Sugar*

Preheat oven to 350 degrees. Help grandchildren wash their hands before working with food.

Place a sheet of wax paper before each grandchild to use as a work surface. Hand each grandchild a triangle of crescent roll. Tell them that this represents the cloth that Jesus was wrapped in when He was laid in the tomb. Give each grandchild a marshmallow to represent Jesus.

Place a bowl with (warm, not hot) melted margarine in front of your grandchildren and let them dip their marshmallow in it. Explain that the margarine represents the oil that was used to protect and preserve Jesus's body.

Prepare another bowl with cinnamon and sugar. Let each grandchild roll the marshmallow representing Jesus in the mixture. Tell them the cinnamon and sugar represent the spices that were used to anoint Jesus's body for burial.

Wrap the coated marshmallow tightly in the crescent roll. Pinch the sides together, making sure that the dough is completely sealed. Let this step represent the wrapping of Jesus's body after His death.

Place the wrapped marshmallows on a cookie sheet and place in the oven. Bake 10 to 12 minutes at 350 degrees. The oven represents the tomb, while the baking time symbolizes the three days that Christ was in the tomb.

When the rolls have cooled slightly, have the grandchildren open their rolls (grave cloth). They will discover that the marshmallow (representing Jesus) is gone. Christ has risen!

Some Grand-Bunny Loves Me
Crafty Ideas for Younger Grandkids

When love and skill work together, expect a masterpiece.
—JOHN RUSKIN

Sew Delightful!

If you are a busy grandma with sewing talent, you can still stitch up a spring frock for your younger granddaughters in a short amount of time. Check out your fabric store for preprinted-pattern fabric. Yes, that's right; you don't even have to buy the pattern. They make easy-to-sew designs for all seasons, so you're sure to find an Easter bunny print. If you're an accomplished seamstress, you may want to look for patterns and fabrics designed by Daisy Kingdom. Granddaughters love these dresses because they twirl and also because Grandma made them. Younger grandsons will be envious, so you may have to purchase an easy shirt pattern and sew a simple shirt using a popular fabric design. Imagine how thrilled they will be to receive a box with these "sew delightful" gifts!

Knit or Crochet for Some Bunny

If sewing is not your hobby, find other ways to create Easter memories. Some grandmas like to crochet or knit. Try crocheting or knitting bunnies, Easter baskets, or purses.

Other Ways to Create Easter Memories

- Mail a cake mix, can of icing, Easter cupcake papers, and some jellybeans. Enlist Mom and Dad's help to bake cupcakes with the grandkids. Sometimes, half the battle is having the supplies available. Mom will appreciate not having to go out and purchase these items.

- E-mail an electronic Easter card.

- Order an Easter cookie bouquet to be delivered to your grandchildren's home.

- Check Web sites for Easter craft ideas for children.

- Write a bunny tale for your grandchildren.

- Cut out woodcrafts and send to older grandchildren to paint.

- Pack an Easter egg coloring kit, along with a videotape of you coloring eggs. If the kit doesn't include directions for boiling eggs, tuck in written instructions for egg boiling. (No kidding! This nutritional tradition is going by the wayside.) You can't mail the eggs you boiled, but you can make deviled eggs or egg salads. Include recipes for those dishes, too, and write a note about how yummy they are.

- Be creative and use your talents to connect with your grandchildren in your unique, memorable way.

Easter Egg Hunt to Go
Hosting a Long-Distance Egg Hunt

You and your grandchildren are separated by miles and miles. Yet it's been a tradition through the generations to have an Easter egg hunt at Grandma and Grandpa's. This calls from some ingenuity. What is a long-distance grandma to do?

- Schedule an egg hunt for when you can visit—before or after Easter Sunday. Flexibility is the name of the game when families live miles apart. The world doesn't come to an end if celebrations can't be held on the exact holiday. Purchase plastic eggs and candy after you arrive at your grandkids' home to reduce the chance of squishing or melting candies.

- Pack and fill plastic eggs in Styrofoam cartons. Placing several dozen in a bigger box to mail when visiting is out of the question. Your adult children or older grandkids will be glad to hide the eggs for the younger children. Ask them to make a videotape, take some digital photos that can be e-mailed, or mail a one-time-use camera so they'll be sure to have film.

Easter Dinner via Long Distance
Sharing Traditional Recipes

"Grandma, why do we cut the ends off the ham before baking?"
I asked, assuming it had to do with flavor.
"Why, so it'd fit inside my pan," she said.

—Unknown

What are the favorite family recipes that are synonymous with Easter dinner—ham, turkey, chicken and noodles? Keep tradition alive by mailing copies of your family's recipes to your adult children and grandchildren. I'm sure you have your own traditional dishes that you prepare for Easter. But here's a copy of one of my favorites—our homemade noodle recipe. Share it with your children and grandchildren who can't be home this Easter. Better yet, if they do get to visit, enlist their help in mixing, rolling, and cutting the noodles. Pass on the tradition.

homemade noodles

- *1 egg*
- *2 tablespoons milk*
- *½ teaspoon salt*
- *1 cup flour*

Multiply the recipe for every three people you plan to serve. Beat together egg, salt, and milk. Add the flour. Roll out the dough as thin as possible on a floured surface, using a rolling pin. Let the grandkids help by taking turns rolling out the dough.

Air-dry the noodle dough. (Allow two hours or longer—wait until the noodles look dry.) Then cut the dough into rectangular shapes, stack the rectangles, and slice very thin. (I use a pizza cutter; it makes noodle cutting easy, and the grandkids love it!)

Heat two quarts of broth to a rolling boil in a large pan. Use six quarts of broth for nine people. Add one teaspoon of salt to the broth for each batch of noodles. Add more if needed—season to taste. (Hint: You may add canned chicken broth if you run low on the broth from your hen or turkey.

Adjust the salt content though. You won't have to add as much salt with canned broth. Another trick is to add up to a quart of water to the broth from your hen or turkey.)

Drop the noodles in a few at a time, keeping the broth boiling. Don't be concerned about the extra flour on the noodles; it will thicken the broth, making the noodles nice and creamy. Turn the heat down to medium and continue stirring frequently. Boil the noodles for ten minutes.

Reduce the heat to low and simmer for another ten minutes, cooking until the noodles are tender. Grandmas have to be taste-testers. You'll know when they are ready. Enjoy!

Showers of Springtime Stories
Books for Easter and Spring

Listening to Grandpa or Grandma read a story by Web camera or video is the next best thing to being there.

—LD Grandma Janet Teitsort

Shower your grandchildren with many good books during this springtime season! Here are a few of my favorites:

The Rabbit and the Promise Sign by Pat Day-Bivins and Philip Dale Smith, illustrated by Donna Brooks (FaithWorks), is a beautiful fictional tale. It is the story of a rabbit that waited with Jesus in the Garden of Gethsemane and was given the promise sign. The book is geared toward four- to eight-year-olds, but all ages will enjoy this delightful book. Include a stuffed bunny with any of the rabbit books. That will be sure to bring a smile!

The Best Thing about Easter by Christine Harder Tangvald

(Standard Publishing) is the perfect book for Easter. This book touches on the fun things of Easter, such as coloring Easter eggs, but it also teaches in a simple manner the true meaning of Easter. This book is another good one for four- to eight-year-olds.

I Wonder . . . Did Jesus Have a Pet Lamb? by Janette Oke, illustrated by Corbert Gauthier (Bethany Backyard) is a book that explores the childhood of Jesus. The springtime scenes of Jesus playing with his pet lamb makes this book ideal to share during this season.

The Velveteen Rabbit by Margery Williams, illustrated by William Nicholson (Doubleday Books for Young Readers), is a classic that you don't want your grandchildren to miss. The story about a toy rabbit that longs to be real will touch your heart. This book is a winner for all ages, even adults.

Fluffy Grows a Garden (Hello Reader Level 3) by Kate McMullan and illustrated by Mavis Smith (Cartwheel Books—Scholastic Imprint) is another winner in the Fluffy series. Fluffy, the classroom guinea pig, learns about gardening and how insects can be helpful. When you mail a copy of this book to your grandchildren, be sure to include a packet of carrot seeds.

The Trellis and the Seed: A Book of Encouragement for All Ages by Jan Karon and illustrated by Robert Gantt Steele (Viking Books) is a wonderful book that will encourage your grandchild's heart as well as yours.

Robin's Home by Jeannine Atkins and illustrated by Candace Whitman (Farrar, Straus and Giroux BYR) teaches about robins and provides a fun bird-watching activity. After your grandkids read this book, have Mom and Dad help them cut some yarn and place on the branches of a tree. Then have them watch to see if the robins will use the yarn to build their nest.

Puddles, Puddles Everywhere!
Rainy-Day Activities

Rain, rain, go away,
Come again another day;
Little Johnny wants to play.

—"RAIN"

Showers are sure to share center stage with the sun and the wind this month. Rest assured that the rain is playing a big part in the spring production of flowers and greenery.

Care Packages

Prepare a care package for those rainy days that keep your grandchildren indoors.

- Mail a box of brightly colored markers, crayons, coloring books, and sketch pads to your grandchildren.

- Send a box of craft supplies. Look around your home for odds and ends of craft materials: old necklaces or beads (if your grandchildren are old enough to use these items), Styrofoam plates, cotton balls, colorful craft chenille sticks, glue sticks, fabric and trim scraps, and bits of yarn or ribbon. Package all the rainy-day supplies in a shoebox and mail.

Noah's Ark

Since this is the month of April showers, don't forget to share the story of Noah's Ark!

- Choose one of the many storybook versions for your younger grandchildren.

- Share the story of Noah's Ark from God's Word with the older grandkids.

- Point out Genesis 2:5–6 and the fact that until the time Noah entered the ark it had never rained.

- Purchase one of the many novelty items available and treat your grandkids. Choose among a replica of the ark, animals, jewelry, tea sets, music boxes, key rings, and coloring books.

- Check out the fabric department for Noah's Ark prints and novelty buttons.

- Mail boxes of animal crackers to younger grandchildren. Include some white paper plates, a glue stick, and markers or crayons. Instruct them to draw a rainbow on the top half of the plate, blue water on the bottom, and an ark in the center. Then glue some of the animal crackers by the ark. Remind them not to eat the crackers with glue on them, but they can eat the crackers they don't glue. Yum, yum! What fun!

Promise Books and Letters

Rainbows remind us of God's covenant promise with mankind— that He will not destroy the earth again by flood. They also make us think of all God's promises contained in His Word.

- Present your grandchild with an age-appropriate promise book, which contains Scripture references for specific circumstances. These little books are inexpensive, encouraging, and available in both Christian and secular bookstores.

- Collect promise scriptures that speak to your family situations. E-mail them to your older grandchildren and tell them you are praying that verse for them or for another family member by inserting their name in the verse and making it personal.

In God We Trust
Military Grandparenting Tips

I guess grandkids keep our eyes functioning, making all those tears.
—JEAN FLORA GLICK

When our grandchildren join the military and serve their nation at home or abroad, we grandparents get misty-eyed with pride and shed a few fearful tears. Here are some tips of comfort:

- Place your military grandkids in God's care daily, praying for their safety and success. Leave them there. God has big hands. If you find you've begun to worry about them again, then place them in God's hands once more. Eventually, you'll get better at leaving them there.

- Choose one of the search engines on the Internet and check Web sites for military families. There are more than 1.7 million sites that will give you suggestions and comfort. Although there is little mention of grandparents on the sites, the information is for family, and you're a part of family! Maybe you'll even want to contribute a grandparent hint for the Web site. After all, we're in this together!

- Take comfort in and claim the following scripture for your family: "But from everlasting to everlasting the LORD's love is with those who fear him, and his righteousness with their children's children—with those who keep his covenant and remember to obey his precepts" (Psalm 103:17–18).

Grand Tip of the Month
The Promise of Easter Is Found in Every Rainbow!

Whenever the rainbow appears in the clouds,
I will see it and remember the everlasting covenant
between God and all living creatures of every kind on the earth.

—GENESIS 9:16

When packing cookies to mail to college or military grandkids, use a metal tin. Place paper towels between layers of cookies. This will keep them from crumbling.

Recording the Legacy

Date_____

Long-distance activity/project _____

_____

Here's what my grandkids said_____

_____

Date_____

Long-distance activity/project _____

_____

Here's what my grandkids said_____

_____

Date_____

Long-distance activity/project _____

Here's what my grandkids said_____

_____

Notes

Children's children are a crown to the aged,
and parents are the pride of their children.
—PROVERBS 17:6

may

Spring is in her glory! She's all dressed up in her finest as if awaiting prom night. Spring dances, graduations, end-of-school programs, Mother's Day, Memorial Day, baseball, softball, and planting season provide us with many opportunities to grandparent by long distance. Grab a pen or your computer keyboard—long distant grandparenting awaits! The choice is yours: how will you be a part of these important moments in your grandchild's life?

Tea for Two
Long-Distance Tea Party
Fill a cup of it for me!
—JAMES WHITCOMB RILEY

Do you want to dress up and have an old-fashioned Victorian tea party, but you can't visit a tearoom? Then try it via long distance. My friend Margaret Anne Huffman, in her book *Everyday Prayers for Grandmothers* (Dimensions for Living), shared how she bought two matching tea sets and mailed one to her granddaughter. What a great idea!

Take it a step or two further, and you can do an entire tea party long distance.

- Buy two matching tea sets or teacups.

- Mail one to your grandkids and you keep the other.

- Include some fancy napkins, Scripture tea bags, and dainty cookies.

- Set a date and invite your grandkids to have a tea party with you.

- Connect with them via Web camera. Not possible? Then mail a one-time-use camera, or have Mom and Dad use the digital camera and e-mail photos. Where there's a will, there's a way!

Dance the Night Away
Sharing Proms—Long-Distance Style

There she stood, my beautiful granddaughter, dressed for the prom. I thought, how can this be? Just yesterday she was playing dress-up.

—Grandma Zelpha Byard

Little girls who once dreamed of being Cinderella grow up and dance the night away at the high-school prom. Young men are transformed into handsome princes to serve as their escorts for this special night. Grandparents want to share in these special events, but the miles separate us. Here are some tips on how to connect with your prom-going grandkids, in spite of the distance.

- Use a digital camera and have Mom and Dad e-mail photos immediately.

- Print the photos and put them in a grandparent brag book to share with friends.

- Purchase that Web camera and share a special phone call. Start using it for this very special night!

- Write a letter or send an e-mail, sharing about your prom. Ask your grandchildren to tell you all about their special evening.

Hey, Mom! A Package for Me!
Springtime Care Packages

I'm excited when I get a package from Grandma and Grandpa. I always wonder what it is. It's really fun when I get something from them.
—TOMMY RICHARDSON, AGE 10

Sunny days are here again, and it's time to send a care package to the grandkids. The miles may prevent you from kissing those boo-boos or skinned knees, but try this:

- Choose some cool Band-Aids that Mom may not buy because they're more expensive. A touch of Grandma and Grandpa's love can bring quick healing.

- Pack some sunglasses to shield younger grandkids' eyes. Teen grandkids may want to pick out their own "cool shades," so just mail a gift card.

- Include heavy-duty sunscreen to protect against sunrays. You might include sunless tanning lotion for older teens. Stress the importance of tanning the safe way.

- Select some fun sun visors or caps.

- Purchase gift certificates if you want to treat grandkids to play clothes or sandals. They love getting to choose. Moms will probably be happy to pick something out for infant grandchildren.

Old MacDonald Had a Farm
Sharing Rural Life with City-Dwelling Grandkids

A child on a farm sees a plane fly overhead and dreams of a faraway place. A traveler on the plane sees the farmhouse . . . and dreams of home.

—Carl Burns

You may live in a rural area—even on a farm. Perhaps your children went off to college, earned degrees, and then moved to the city to find a job in their respective fields of education. If that is the case, then don't miss the opportunity to share with your grandchildren the wonders of rural living.

In the spring when new life abounds with the birth of farm animals and spring planting, share the events in the following ways:

- Videotape the playful animals from calves to kittens, and mail the videotape to your grandkids.

- Snap photos of spring planting in progress. (Be sure to include Grandpa in the picture!)

- Mail miniature toy tractors and plastic farm animals. Include a letter explaining farm life.

- See book selections for this month for ideal farm books and movies.

Connecting Spiritually
Gardening Fun

This is what the kingdom of God is like.
A man scatters seed on the ground. Night and day,
whether he sleeps or gets up, the seed sprouts and grows,
though he does not know how.

—MARK 4:26–27

Gardening or planting must be very near to the heart of God, for Jesus told many parables about the sower, seeds, plants, and harvestings. As a gardener or farmer goes about planting and harvesting tasks, the parables of Christ come alive with meaning. Begin to cultivate within your grandchildren a love and respect for the cycle of planting, nourishing, and harvesting.

- Mail small, inexpensive gardening tools. Include kneeling pads, gardening gloves, and maybe a hat.

- Send a book on square-foot or patio-pot gardening.

- Purchase packets of easy-to-grow pumpkin seeds. Your grandkids can use the pumpkins for autumn projects. Gourd seeds are fun too!

- Surprise your grandkids with the ingredients for this fun dessert (except the milk, of course!):

down-to-earth surprise

- *1 package instant vanilla pudding*
- *Milk (add amount listed on pudding box)*
- *1 package chocolate cookies*

- *1 package Gummi Worms*
- *Clear plastic punch cups*

Mix pudding and milk according to directions on the box. Pour a thick layer of pudding into each cup. Place a Gummi Worm on top of layer. Add another layer of pudding. Top with crushed chocolate cookies. (Hint: Place chocolate cookies in a gallon plastic storage bag. Crush with rolling pin or use the bottom of a plastic glass to smash them into crumbs.)

Planting Seeds of Thoughtfulness
Celebrating May Holidays

Train up a child in the way he should go; and when he is old, he will not depart from it.
—PROVERBS 22:6 KJV

Mother's Day

Special! That's how you want Mom to feel on Mother's Day. Encourage your grandchildren to pamper her, as well as give her a purchased or homemade gift. How they celebrate this day will depend on their age and Dad's cooperation.

Advise grandkids to put some time and thought into their gift selections. A thoughtful gift considers Mom's personality. What type of gift would she like? Some moms like fresh-cut flowers; others see them as a waste. Some moms are thrilled to receive a gift certificate, while others think you've taken the easy way out. Remind them to know their mom!

Here are some inexpensive suggestions that even a young grandchild can do with a little help from Dad:

- Color a picture for Mom.

- Purchase her favorite candy bar. Every mother needs chocolate; give one from each child.

- Give Mom a "One Golden Hour of Time" certificate. Remind the grandkids that means they can't interrupt her!

- Give a promise certificate that guarantees "No Yackety-Yak or Talking Back" for one entire day.

Memorial Day (Decoration Day)

The grandkids may only know Memorial Day as a holiday that signifies the beginning of summer. Perhaps you heard your parents or grandparents refer to it as Decoration Day. Maybe you wore a red poppy in honor of those who died in service to our country. This custom was inspired by Moina Michael's poem, written in 1915:

> *We cherish too, the poppy red*
> *That grows on fields where valor led;*
> *It seems to signal to the skies*
> *That blood of heroes never dies.*

Not too many years ago, American families not only paid homage to war heroes on this day, but also visited the cemeteries and decorated the graves of their loved ones. Today, due to families being separated by miles of interstate, this custom has ceased. Sadly, we've also lost the sharing of oral history that accompanied the practice. This calls for finding new ways of preserving this special day of remembrance.

- Research online with your grandchild how Memorial Day started. Much history surrounds this holiday!

- Use the postal service or e-mail a patriotic poem or prayer to your older grandkids, reminding them to pray for our nation and our troops.

- Purchase a patriotic coloring book, crayons, and stickers to send to younger grandkids.

- Prepare a CD or photo album of ancestors, along with a written history, and send to each adult child to share with the grandkids. Make one for yourself too. When your extended family gets together, pull out the album and share about your ancestors. Sharing family genealogy gives us a strong identity and bridges the generations.

Getting to Know You
Blending Families Smoothly

Love is always open arms. If you close your arms about love, you will find that you are left holding only yourself.

—LEO BUSCAGLIA

Here are a few more tips on blending your mixed batch of grandkids with grace:

- Give all (biological and bonus) grandchildren a balanced amount of your time and attention. Children respond to fairness.

- Share phone calls with all grandkids. Getting to know a grandchild takes both quantity and quality time.

- Mail notes and cards for all your younger grandkids in one family in a large manila envelope. The idea is not to save postage, but that the letters will all arrive on the same day. You don't want any little one feeling left out because his or her letter didn't arrive.

A May Basket of Ideas
Books and Activities

Let us read and let us dance—two amusements
that will never do any harm to the world.

—VOLTAIRE

When you set up the camcorder or plug in the cassette recorder to read to your grandchildren, share a few memories. Be sure to tell the tales that might not get told unless you take the time to tell them! Talk to each other. Don't let distance keep you from sharing! Enjoy these books and activities to celebrate the month of May.

The Honeybee and the Robber by Eric Carle (Scholastic) has moveable pictures. Share with your grandkids if you ever went barefoot in the spring. Did the grass tickle your toes? Did you ever step on a honeybee? Tell them about it. Grandchildren today seldom go barefoot because they're on the go, live in a city, or have lots of sandals.

Honeybees love flowers. Do you remember making tissue flowers? Children delight in making these, and today there are all colors of tissues on the market. How fun! Here are some easy-to-follow directions:

tissue flowers

You will need:

- *Boxes of colored tissues*
- *Child-safe scissors*
- *Pipe cleaners*

Do:

1. *Unfold one tissue; fold in half, then fold again.*

2. *Trim along the folded edge (two sides).*

3. *Gather or pleat in the center, wrap the pipe cleaner tightly around it, and twist.*

4. *Gently pick tissue sheets apart, lifting upward toward the center.*

5. *Presto! You have just created a blossom!*

Town Mouse, Country Mouse by Jan Brett (Putnam Publishing Group) compares the benefits of country living with city living and vice versa.

Charlotte's Web by E. B. White (Harper & Row) is a fun book about farm animals. This one is available on video. In fact, browse among the videos and DVDs; there are several cute videos depicting life on the farm.

Are You My Mother? by P. D. Eastman (Random House) is about a little bird that has gotten separated from his mother and is searching for her. Include a show-and-tell book about birds, a how-to book on making bird houses, inexpensive binoculars, and the ingredients and following recipe for Tasty Bird's Nest:

tasty bird's nest

- *1 can chow-mein noodles*
- *1 package butterscotch morsels*
- *1 package jellybean miniatures*

    Place the butterscotch morsels in a glass baking dish. Melt morsels in the microwave for three to five minutes. Stir in the noodles, coating them with the melted butterscotch morsels. Form the mixtures into round nests, denting the centers. Add the jellybeans—a neat, nesty snack!

The Little Red Hen (several versions available) is an ageless story that teaches kids about doing their share of the work. Mom will love you for reminding her crew to pull their own weight. The story fits nicely with planting season too.

The Mother's Day Mice by Eve Bunting (Clarion Books) is a fun read for Mother's Day.

Blueberries for Sal by Robert McCloskey (Puffin Books) is another "berry" book. Ever go berry picking? Tell your grandchildren about it! Did you eat more than you picked? What did your family do with the berries? Have you ever made jellies and jam?

- Videotape yourself making jam or jelly, as well as reading the "berry" books on tape.

- Pour some of the homemade jam or jelly in some plastic jars and mail with the video.

- Mail a box of Sure Jell and ask Mom to assist the grandkids in making their own jam and jelly.

- Send the following story, "Strawberry Jam," along with some strawberry jelly packs (ask to purchase a few at your local restaurant). Miniature gourmet jars of jelly are available at Christmas time in gift sets. These can be purchased ahead and kept back with May activities in mind. Purchase some gourmet biscuits from your deli to mail with the story.

Strawberry Jam

Once upon a time, there lived a teeny-tiny woman in a teeny-tiny town. She was very lonesome. She thought, *I will invite some friends to join me for a picnic.* "Let's see," she said. "What will I need?" Since the teeny-tiny woman lived by herself, she often talked to herself just to hear the sound of a voice.

Opening her cupboard, she noticed that she didn't have any bread. She decided right then and there that she would spend her morning baking some fresh bread. She took down her teeny-tiny bowl and set it on her teeny-tiny table. She measured out some water and yeast and then added some flour and other ingredients. She soon had a big ball of bread dough. She kneaded it with her hands until it became smooth and shiny, then she formed it into loaves. Her teeny-tiny kitchen was nice and warm; she knew that the bread would soon rise. When the bread doubled in size, she would place it in her teeny-tiny oven.

An hour passed, and the teeny-tiny woman checked on the dough. Sure enough, it was just right, and she put it in her teeny-tiny oven. Soon her teeny-tiny kitchen smelled heavenly as the aroma of the bread filled the air. A short while later, she had several loaves of teeny-tiny bread lined up on her table. She sliced the bread into teeny-tiny slices.

"But what will I put on the bread for my guests? I know!" she said, talking aloud to herself. "I will go pick some teeny-tiny strawberries and make some jam."

The teeny-tiny woman put on her teeny-tiny bonnet to keep the hot sun off of her teeny-tiny face, and she went out to her teeny-tiny strawberry patch. She filled her teeny-tiny basket with the teeny-tiny strawberries and went back into her teeny-tiny cottage. She set right to work and made the most delicious strawberry jam. She couldn't help but think how much her friends and neighbors would love the strawberry jam on her teeny-tiny slices of bread. "I think I'd better sample some, just to be sure it's tasty," and that is just what she did. "Ummm," she said. "This is scrumptious, if I do say so myself."

There was only one thing left for her to do. She went to her teeny-tiny telephone and called all her teeny-tiny friends and neighbors. "Ant, would you like to go on a picnic tomorrow and have some of my teeny-tiny bread with just a teeny-tiny bit of strawberry jam?"

"Would I?" asked the ant. "You know how I love picnics, but no one ever invites me. I always have to crash outdoor parties."

"You poor thing," said the teeny-tiny woman, "Consider yourself invited. Bye for now, see you tomorrow."

In a short while, she had called ten different guests. She decided that they would stroll over by the teeny-tiny pond, which was located in the teeny-tiny town's park. "Why, we'll just sit under the teeny-tiny shade trees and have our teeny-tiny picnic," and they did. When they were finished, she thought, *What could I do with these leftover slices of bread? Everyone here is so full.*

Then she had a clever idea. She packed her teeny-tiny bread in a teeny-tiny box and took it to the teeny-tiny post office. She gave it to the teeny-tiny postman and said, "Please address this to anyone you know who might enjoy hearing from a teeny-tiny woman and having some of my teeny-tiny bread and jam."

The teeny-tiny postman said, "I sure will!" Then the teeny-tiny postman thought of YOU!

- Videotape yourself making bread from scratch—if you like to do that type of thing. If not, ask Mom to purchase a bag of frozen yeast dough so the kids can bake bread when reading *The Little Red Hen*. Mom and Dad might even have a bread maker. Yum! I can almost smell the aroma of homemade bread baking!

- Wait for a visit and make bread from scratch or frozen dough with your grandkids. They'll love it! The experience might turn your hair white. After all, flour seems to go everywhere. (Now, what did you think I meant?)

Grand Tip of the Month
Put Life on Pause, then Hit Record.
Share Memories from the Past!

Take time to form those family ties into everlasting knots.
—LD Grandma Janet Teitsort

Scrapbook by the month—keep an ongoing photo album beside your computer. Print e-mailed photos as soon as you receive them and place them in your album. Crop wasted background and focus on your grandchild! Make monthly collages of photos instead of placing one or two photos on a page. Grandparents have too many photos to scrapbook in that manner!

Recording the Legacy

Date_____

Long-distance activity/project _____

_____

Here's what my grandkids said_____

_____

Date_____

Long-distance activity/project _____

_____

Here's what my grandkids said_____

_____

Date_____

Long-distance activity/project _____

_____

Here's what my grandkids said_____

_____

Notes

_____

_____

_____

_____

_____

_____

_____

_____

_____

_____

_____

_____

_____

_____

_____

_____

_____

_____

_____

_____

_____

_____

_____

june

In June, spring bows out and summer sweeps in. Branches laden with gracious, green leaves dance in summer's premier, inviting us outside.

The Teddy Bears' Picnic
Picnic in a Box

It's fun to have a picnic on the playground by the woods.
—LAINIE RICHARDSON, AGE 7

Ask your grandkids to invite their teddy bears to a picnic. Include some cute bear-shaped cookies in your mailing. You might even want to send a sing-along tape of the song "The Teddy Bears' Picnic" (Warner Brothers) or the book *The Teddy Bears' Picnic* by Jimmy Kennedy, illustrated by Prue Theobalds (Peter Bedrick Books).

- Pack and mail a small box with plastic tableware, paper napkins, plates, and tablecloth.

- Send a one-time-use camera for Mom to use or with instructions that each child gets to take a certain number of pictures.

- Include a cool summer drink mix.

- Purchase a "Have a Nice Day" handheld bread press. These nifty presses imprint a design on a bread slice. The imprint adds a special touch to the sandwiches. The presses can be found in the kitchen department of most stores and are fun to use.

June Bugs and Beary Good Books
June Book Selections

Make new friends, but keep the old.
One is silver and the other is gold.
—Unknown

The following books will fit right in with the arrival of summer. Bugs are about as close to nature as you can get. Also, if you go with the teddy bears' picnic theme, you'll want to take advantage of all the bear books on the market. Try these delightful books to read on videotape, cassette tape, Web camera, or phone. (Be sure to mail grandkids a copy of the book so they can read along—it also helps build their library.) Get Grandpa involved, and have him read a book or two. Along with these classics, you can also check out new books on the market.

Brown Bear, Brown Bear, What Do You See? written by Bill Martin Jr. and illustrated by Eric Carle (Henry Holt & Co.)

Polar Bear, Polar Bear, What Do You Hear? written by Bill Martin Jr. and illustrated by Eric Carle (Scholastic)

The Grouchy Ladybug by Eric Carle (Scholastic)

The Honeybee and the Robber by Eric Carle (Scholastic)

The Very Busy Spider by Eric Carle (Scholastic)

The Very Quiet Cricket by Eric Carle (Scholastic)

The Very Hungry Caterpillar by Eric Carle (Scholastic)

Winnie the Pooh books by A. A. Milne

The Berenstain Bears by Stan and Jan Berenstain (Random House)

The Little Bear series by Else H. Minarik (Harper & Row)

Goldilocks and the Three Bears (several versions available) Don't forget this all-time favorite.

June Is Bursting with Celebrations!
Activities for Holidays and Parties
Grandma and I love parties!
—SARAH TEITSORT, AGE 5

Graduation

Proms are over, and it is graduation time! Although we try, sometimes we grandparents feel unsure about what to give our young-adult grandkids. We tend to think that big events call for big gifts, when, in fact, the more momentous the occasion, the more meaningful the gift should be. Here are a couple of ideas:

- Give monetary gifts to graduating grandkids—they'll be appreciated, especially with future expenses looming on the horizon.

- Add to the monetary gift a special letter or an heirloom of significant meaning.

Flag Day

Grandparents, here's your chance to plant the seeds of patriotism in young hearts. Using the Internet or library, do one or more of the following:

- Gather info regarding when Flag Day was first recognized.

- Share the proper care of the United States flag.

- Research the history and design of the first American flag.

- Mail some American flag stickers or a package of toothpick-size American flags.

- Sew (or buy) some patriotic play clothes.

- Craft some American memorabilia: earrings, T-shirts, wooden cutouts—whatever fits your budget, time, and the ages of your grandchildren.

- Spiritually connect with your grandkids using 2 Chronicles 7:14: "If my people, who are called by my name, will humble themselves and pray and seek my face and turn from their wicked ways, then will I hear from heaven and will forgive their sin and will heal their land."

- Challenge your grandkids to pray for our nation, our leaders, our armed forces, and for peace throughout the world.

Father's Day

Here are some tips to share with your grandchildren on how to celebrate this day with their special dad. These one-of-a-kind gifts teach children the importance of putting thought and preparation into their gift giving. Homemade is always best—the key ingredient is love!

- Ask Mom to help them make a personalized T-shirt. Mom can guide small hands in and out of paint, pressing colorful hand prints onto sweatshirts. The grandkids can also use squeeze bottles of paint and create unique designs.

- Send a cap and small resin ornaments, magnets, and buttons, along with fabric glue. Older grandkids, or younger ones with Mom's help, can glue and create a unique hat for Dad.

- Suggest the grandkids create an "I will help . . ." card, thus giving a part of themselves.

Special Occasions

Weddings, anniversaries, baptisms, piano and dance recitals don't always happen in June, but sometimes they do. Whenever and whatever the special occasion, have someone record it. You can share the special event, even though apart. Be creative: connect through a letter, snapshots, cassette tape, videotape, or Web camera—but do connect!

School Is Out!
Staying in Touch with College Grandkids

Anyone who stops learning is old, whether at twenty or eighty. Anyone who keeps learning stays young. The greatest thing in life is to keep your mind young.

—HENRY FORD

Your college-age grandchild may stay on campus for the summer sessions, travel abroad, take a job in their college town, or work in their hometown. But one thing is certain: if you want to stay connected with them, you need to become a high-tech grandparent. Connecting via e-mail, phone, or cell phone is the way of the world—and especially your college grandkids. Here are some tips to ensure that you stay connected through the summer, whether on or off campus:

- Ask your college grandchild to teach you how to use the on-line Instant Messenger. Then set a daily time to chat with your grandchild. What fun! They'll think Grandma and Grandpa are cool! Does that seem too high tech for you? Then definitely use e-mail.

- Provide phone cards and ask them to call you when they have time to talk—from anywhere. Their schedule is probably busier then yours. But do give them your schedule too.

- Trade cell-phone numbers and share when you have free minutes. Hint: using the same cell phone carrier as your grandkids allows you more free access to each other.

Summer Shape-Up
Physical Fitness

Exercise makes you strong, and it's fun with Grandma!
—HANNAH RICHARDSON, AGE 8

One, two, three, stretch! Summer time is shape-up time! Today's grandparents are into physical fitness. We want to be healthy and live long, productive lives so we can keep up with the grandkids.

We also know more about the role exercise plays in our lives. We want our children and grandchildren to begin their stretch for physical fitness at an early age.

- Buy an exercise video (some include scriptures and songs) to send to your grandchildren. Be sure to check out the market and make an age-appropriate selection. Make a commitment to each other to exercise daily, or at least four times a week. Keep a chart. Reward them and yourself by banking so much money per mile. Then when you get to visit, go on a special outing with the accumulated funds.

- Send older grandkids a CD or tape of their favorite Christian music and invite them to exercise to the music. This provides them with a Christian message while motivating them to "get movin'."

Star Light, Star Bright
Stargazing Activities

Be glad of life because it gives you the chance to love and to work and to play and to look up at the stars.

—Henry Van Dyke

Summer nights are great for stargazing. Toss a blanket on the ground and check out the night sky. What constellations do you see? Share your information.

Thrill a grandchild by calling 1-800-282-3333 and naming a star after them (thirty-five spaces or less). The star names will officially appear in a book, *Your Place in the Cosmos*.

Starry Projects

- Make some star cookies; package them between layers of paper towels, and mail.

- Teach the little ones how to draw a star. You can make step-by-step drawings and include them with a letter.

- Mail a package of colored foil stars with some blue or black construction paper. Let them create their own star pictures.

- Research and study constellations with your grandchildren.

- Purchase packets of glow-in-the-dark stars that will adhere to their bedroom ceiling. Suggest Mom and Dad use them to form constellations. (Better check with Mom and Dad first on this one!)

- Write stories starring your grandchildren. Send via snail mail or e-mail. On each page, draw a star and write a quality that you recognize in your grandchild. Everyone loves praise, and too often we don't take time to say it.

A Starring Book

The Drinking Gourd by Ferdinand N. Monjo, illustrated by Fred Brenner (Harper Collins). This wonderful book is about the Underground Railroad and how slaves used the Big Dipper to find their way north to freedom. This story will go perfectly with your stargazing, as well as provide a history lesson.

Connecting Spiritually
Our Omnipresent God

Great is the L ORD and most worthy of praise; his greatness no one can fathom.
—P SALM 145:3

As you stargaze with your grandchildren, teach them that God is omnipresent—present everywhere at the same time. Stress that the same stars are shining in the same night sky where you and your grandchildren live. The same God is watching over both households and can be present in both locations at the same time. Wow!

- Introduce your grandchild to Isaiah 47:13–15. Search the Scriptures and find other verses that warn us not to plan our lives by our horoscopes or by what a fortune teller has to say. Help your grandchild to become grounded in the Word.

- Research with your older grandkids the difference between astronomy and astrology.

Grand Tip of the Month

Even if You're Miles Apart, Remember:
Your Family Can Be Near in Heart!

A happy family is but an earlier heaven.

—JOHN BOWRING

Save quarters and give a roll of them to your college-age grandchild when he or she comes for a visit (they're too heavy to mail). They can use them for the laundry and snack machines at school.

Recording the Legacy

Date_____

Long-distance activity/project _____

_____

Here's what my grandkids said_____

_____

Date_____

Long-distance activity/project _____

_____

Here's what my grandkids said_____

_____

Date_____

Long-distance activity/project _____

_____

Here's what my grandkids said_____

_____

Notes

_____

_____

_____

_____

_____

_____

_____

_____

_____

_____

_____

_____

_____

_____

_____

_____

*Other things may change us, but
we start and end with family.*
—ANTHONY BRANDT

july

Gardens have been planted, homes have been spruced up, and now it's time to relax. All thoughts turn to vacation. Who will visit whom and when? Before you or your extended family begin to plan, ask for God's guidance and protection upon your trip.

On the Road Again
Travel Packs for Grandkids

After the grandkids visit, a long-distance grandma won't wash the handprints off the windows for a long, long time.
—LD GRANDMA JANET TEITSORT

If your extended family is coming to visit you and the trip involves several states, help Mom and Dad prepare for the grandkids' travel adventure.

Interstate Travel

- Send a map of the United States or the country that the grandkids will be traveling in. Mail it a week or two ahead of their planned departure.

91

- Purchase backseat travel books for the grandkids (search on-line stores for a huge variety). These books, filled with activities, serve a dual purpose: they teach about the states and keep children entertained. Rand McNally has some good ones, but there are many available.

- Check out travel games on the market. Good places to find these games are in bookstores, online bookstores, airport gift shops, and gas stations.

- Provide headsets for older grandkids (if they don't already have them). If they already have headsets, a new CD will bring a smile—that is, if you check with Mom about something they'd like. When the miles get long, offer a reprieve from too much togetherness!

- Do your grandchildren have a portable DVD player in their car? If so, check with Mom and Dad about some movie ideas, and mail the grandkids a new release or favorite DVD to watch during the trip.

- Invent your own "I Spy" travel checklist. Compile a list of twenty items, such as places, travel signs, cars, and trucks. Give each grandchild his or her own age-appropriate list. This way, everyone's a winner! Have a treat for when they arrive. List cows in a field and McDonald's for younger grandkids. Give the older ones certain models of cars and historical markers to find.

- Take advantage of clearance tables and purchase small, inexpensive items of interest for your grandkids. Wrap them individually and mail them prior to their trip. Include a note that says they may unwrap one small gift upon entering a new state, or designate the gift opening by time or miles.

- Include some individually wrapped snacks for when the grandkids get hungry and travel time is too precious to stop.

Air Travel

- Consider purchasing stuffed animal backpacks for younger grandkids. These packs provide storage space for travel books and the comfort of having a cuddly friend with them on the trip. Older grandkids will appreciate age-appropriate backpacks too.

- Give rolling totes (carry-on luggage) for birthday or Christmas gifts. They're perfect for carrying personal possessions through the airports. Some have "I'm going to Grandma's" printed on them. Of course, the older grandkids won't want that, but the little ones will love it—so cute!

To Grandma and Grandpa's House We Go
Things to Do When the Grandkids Visit

Vacations are great! But the fondest memories come from visits to Grandma and Grandpa's house. Spending time together is how we really get to know each other. Time spent together reveals our likes and dislikes; it allows us to reveal our personalities and appreciate one another on a deeper level.

Grandparents, don't take on more than you can handle. But if you're up to it, you may want to invite all the cousins for a visit. Sometimes it's the only time long-distance cousins have to get acquainted. Be sure to enlist some help among the family members.

Plan ahead by cooking and freezing meals in advance. This will give you more time to play with the grandkids.

Fill the time you spend with your grandkids doing imaginative, simple activities, such as the following:

- Dig up worms.
- Go fishing.
- Take a walk.
- Throw pebbles in a stream and watch the ripples.
- Collect rocks along a creek bank.
- Work in the garden.
- Pot some flowers.
- Roast hot dogs.
- Feed the farm animals.
- Cook a meal.
- Make homemade ice cream.
- Bake a pie.
- Bake homemade bread.
- Lie under a shade tree and look up at the sky through the leaves.
- Watch the clouds drift by.
- Catch fireflies.
- Walk to the post office.
- Visit the library, park, or a museum.
- Go shopping.
- Have a picnic.
- Worship together.

If you're feeling creative when the grandkids come to visit, try some of these simple and fun ideas:

- Write your version of a fairy tale in play format, assign parts, create simple costumes, and videotape the entire production. What a memory maker!

- Clean your closets and fill a plastic storage tub with discarded clothing, purses, shoes, and jewelry. Younger grandkids will have a ball playing dress-up when they come to visit.

- Gather odds and ends of dishes from your cabinets or purchase some at a garage sale. The grandkids will delight in using these castoffs for their tea parties or when playing restaurant. (Hint: give three-year-olds and up dry macaroni to stir in a saucepan. They feel like they're really cooking! They can easily spoon the dry pasta onto plates for restaurant play.)

By now you get the idea. Weave into the fabric of your time together the simple things that can be shared—things that make memories and touch the heart.

Camp G & G
Summer Camp at Grandma and Grandpa's

When G'pa Eble laughed he enjoyed it so that everyone around stopped what they were doing to find out what was so funny.

—MONA PLUMER

Call it Camp Grandma & Grandpa, Camp G & G, or Cousins Camp. The grandchildren will love it when you host a special camp just for them. It's a great time to get all the long-distance cousins together so they can get acquainted.

Themes are so fun! Be sure to choose one for your days or week of camp.

Fun Themes and Ideas to Try

- Go patriotic with Camp Red, White, and Blue! Make American flag–themed treats, watch a patriotic movie, and proudly wear red, white, and blue clothes.

- Throw a beach party. If you don't have a pool, an inflatable pool is just fine. For a fun activity, freeze small toys in paper cups and provide each grandchild with a squirt gun. Remove the paper cup and place the iced toy in the swimming pool. Each child squirts their frozen toy until the ice melts and they can retrieve the prize.

- Host a luau. Watch a "how-to-hula" tape and wear grass skirts. Serve pigs in blankets (hot dogs wrapped in biscuits).

- Giddyap with a Western theme! If you don't live on a farm or ranch, see if there's one close by that you can visit. Even better—maybe someone who has a pony will let your grandkids enjoy a ride!

Getting Ready for Camp G & G

- Send invitations to go along with your theme a week or two before the visit. Make your camp coincide with Mom and Dad's visit.

- Shop for supplies at a craft or novelty store that will add to your theme. (Hint: shop Dollar Tree or similar stores for inexpensive but nifty supplies).

- Buy packages of white T-shirts (boys' and men's department) to make camp shirts. Prewash and have the kids paint with shaped sponges or tie-dye. You can also decorate caps or sun visors to vary the routine from year to year.

- Order or purchase prepackaged craft kits.

- Balance out the day with crafts, physical activities, and downtime. You don't want too much of any one thing. Sample day: Crafts, lunch, hike, story time, dinner, outside games (tag), baths, movie to wind down before bedtime.

- Stock up on movies and books (the local library is great— no cost!) for quiet time.

Camp G & G Essentials

As you plan for the grandkids' arrival, remember: camp just wouldn't be camp without some of these:

- Bubbles
- Crafts
- Hikes/walks
- Picnics
- S'mores
- Hot dog roast

Alternative: Try a Grand Camp

If Camp G & G is out of the question and you can afford it, consider taking some of your grandchildren on vacation with you. You can rotate the grandkids by the years based on their ages. Grand Camps are springing up across America. You can generally take two or more grandchildren (ages seven through twelve), and the cost is around three hundred dollars per person. LifeQuest Ministries offers two such camps: one is in Colorado (Pinecrest in Florissant, Colorado), and another is in Missouri (Windermere

Conference Center in Lake of the Ozarks, Missouri). For more information, e-mail: lifequest@gbronline.com or visit their Web site: www.elderquest.org. These Grand Camps are designed with both the grandparents and grandchildren in mind, and they promise first-class accommodations.

Togetherness—Family Style
Vacationing with the Extended Family

A family vacation is one where you arrive with five bags, four kids, and seven I-thought-you-packed-its.

—IVERN BALL

Family Togetherness

Extended families, whether separated by a long distance or just a few miles, may want to consider spending some vacation time together each year. Busy lifestyles keep children as separated as do the miles. Today's busy families tend not to visit if plans aren't made. Grandma, keep those family ties strong by suggesting a family vacation either at your home or at an agreed-upon vacation spot.

Vacationing at Grandma and Grandpa's House

When the extended family comes to visit, day trips are a fun way for everyone to spend time together. Grandma, suggest something fun to do.

- Choose from among your state's sightseeing opportunities.

The zoo is always good. Hands-on museums are next in line, along with amusement parks.

- Present each grandchild with a one-time-use camera. They love taking their own photos. You can add a miniphoto album for fun.

Shortening the Distance

- Meet halfway if several families are coming from different states. Mountain village resorts are fun for family get-togethers.

- Stay at a hotel and relax around the pool. Grandma, you've got it made!

Celebrate America!
The Fourth of July

America is a tune. It must be sung together.
—GERALD STANLEY LEE

Family vacations may enable your clan to be together during this bang-up holiday. If not, use some ingenuity and celebrate together in heart, even if apart.

- Share cassette-tape recordings about some Fourth of July celebrations you remember. Be sure to tell about the parade in your town.

- Have Mom and Dad videotape your grandkids if they are participating in a hometown parade.

- Tell them about the games you played on the Fourth of

July—mail or give them the heirloom croquet set in your basement.

- Mail them a gift certificate and suggest they purchase a family game for the Fourth of July.
- Use the Web camera and be together, though apart.
- Remember to send online greeting cards to delight your little ones.
- Call each other or use online Instant Messenger—find a way to share your day!
- Mail the following directions on how to make a flag cake and how to make individualized servings of ice cream:

flag cake

- *1 package white cake mix (any brand)*
- *1 container white frosting*
- *Blue food coloring*
- *Bag of pecans, or foil-wrapped candies*
- *Red candied cherries*

Bake a white cake in an oblong pan. Ice with white frosting, reserving a small amount. Tint the reserved frosting blue. Ice the top left with a small blue rectangle. Arrange thirteen (represents the original colonies) pecans, or foil-wrapped candies, in a circle on the blue. Cut candied cherries in half. Create red stripes on the cake by placing cherries in rows.

ice cream delight

- *2 gallon-size plastic storage bags*
- *Ice (cubed or crushed)*

- *6 tablespoons table salt*
- *¾ cup milk*
- *1½ tablespoons sugar*
- *1 teaspoon vanilla*

Fill one of the gallon bags half full of ice along with table salt. Fill the second gallon bag with the milk, sugar, and vanilla. Place the second bag inside the bag of ice. Shake until solid. This recipe makes enough for one person, so make additional batches for the number of people who want ice cream. Enjoy!

Let Freedom Ring!
Grandkids in the Military

Patriotism is not so much protecting the land of our fathers as preserving the land of our children.

—JOSÉ ORTEGA Y GASSET

Want to encourage a grandson or granddaughter in the military? Then try some of these tips:

- Print address labels with your grandson or granddaughter's military address and post them on a church or work bulletin board. Friends and coworkers will be happy to drop a line of encouragement to them. (Hint: add a note stating that one U.S. postage stamp is sufficient for all American armed forces, even if abroad.)

- Enlist the support of schoolteachers, scout leaders, or church youth leaders to have their class or group write letters to those serving our country.

- Ask your grandchild what their unit can use. Then stir up some support and supplies among your coworkers, friends, community, and church.

- Pray daily for your military grandchild's safety and success.

Sparkling Book Ideas
Story Time

Books are like sparklers; they light up your life.
—LD GRANDMA JANET TEITSORT

Hopefully this summer you will be able to personally read books to your little ones and watch videos together. Whether on tape, Web camera, or in person, continue your book sharing.

- Stay current by checking online bookstores for the latest patriotic books.

- Spend an afternoon browsing in a bookstore or library. You'll be brimming with all kinds of selections.

- Choose books and videos with an outdoor theme or those filled with summer activities.

- Don't ignore the classics; whether books or videos, they're always winners! Try Johanna Spyri's *Heidi* and *Where the Red Fern Grows* by Wilson Rawls. Enjoy!

Connecting Spiritually
Blessings Abound

Cast all your anxiety upon him because he cares for you.
—1 PETER 5:7

The old adage "The only thing certain about life is change itself" is so true. But focus on the positive instead of the negative. View technology as a blessing instead of something too hard to learn. Interact with a grandchild and allow him or her to teach you. Embrace advances in technology as gifts that enable your family to stay connected. Count the blessings of the twenty-first century:

- Interstates and improved roads
- Air travel
- Trains and buses
- Safer and better cars
- Multiphone lines
- Cell phones with photos
- Cameras—digital and web
- E-mail and Web sites
- Online shopping with delivery
- Faster postal services
- Overnight express

Above all—*prayer* and *faith* remain, keeping us anchored in a changing world.

Grand Tip of the Month
Have Fun Baking and Jamming with Your Grandkids!

*The aroma of bread baking always
carries me back to Grandma's house.*

—LD Grandma Janet Teitsort

Grandma, cook up some family favorites, but be sure to add some convenience foods to the menus. You want to have time to enjoy the grandkids. For example, serve French toast sticks instead of stirring up pancake batter.

Recording the Legacy

Date_____

Long-distance activity/project _____

_____

Here's what my grandkids said_____

_____

Date_____

Long-distance activity/project _____

_____

Here's what my grandkids said_____

_____

Date_____

Long-distance activity/project _____

_____

Here's what my grandkids said_____

_____

Notes

_____

_____

_____

_____

_____

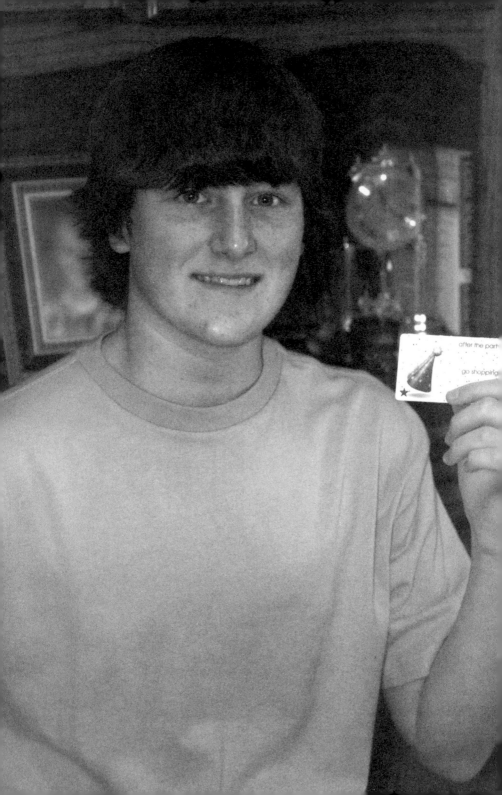

*Grandchildren are God's way of
compensating us for growing old.*
—MARY H. WALDRIP

august

"Summertime, and the living is easy"—so goes the opening line of a song from *Porgy and Bess*. Take advantage of the few remaining days of summer and make some memories with your grandchildren.

Lazy Days of Summer
Memory Makers

*Summer afternoon; to me those have always been the
two most beautiful words in the English language.*
—HENRY JAMES

Just a Swingin'

Summertime is a perfect time to relax and enjoy long, lazy days on a porch swing. Pass down the tradition of "swinging away" the summer with some of these ideas:

- Share memories of the swings you enjoyed as a child (rope, tire, or porch swing).
- Take the grandkids to a park to swing on their next visit. It's an inexpensive memory maker.

- Visit their home and help Dad build a swing set.
- Give a financial gift toward a family swing or play set as a birthday present.

Summer Fairs

County and state fairs in the summer are as American as apple pie. While the miles may make attending these events impossible, you can do the following:

- Let the grandkids ride the mechanical cars and toys at the mall. Have Mom and Dad reserve these novelty rides only for grandparent visits.
- Visit the food court at the mall and choose foods similar to concessions sold at the county fair.
- Make a day trip to an amusement park during a visit with your grandchildren.

Birthday Smiles across the Miles
Celebrating Grand Birthdays

There are three hundred and sixty-four days when you might get un-birthday presents . . . and only one for birthday presents, you know.

—LEWIS CARROLL

Long-distance families can still connect for birthdays. Celebrate multiple-family birthdays—in person—whenever the extended family can get together. If the family can get together twice a year, you can divide the year in half, having a summer and winter celebration. If not, hopefully you can get together for one major birthday party. If you have to, you can celebrate birthdays online via the Web camera.

Between get-togethers, be sure to phone, e-mail electronic cards, or mail birthday cards. A fax machine is great for sending homemade greeting cards and photocopies of snapshots.

When birthdays arrive and you can't be there, try these ideas:

- Splurge on cookie or balloon bouquets.

- Sing "Happy Birthday" over the phone.

- Mail a birthday package, complete with birthday napkins and party supplies.

- Give gift certificates for a favorite restaurant to older grandkids.

- Send a subscription to an age-appropriate magazine. (Hint: before making your selection, check with the parents first and then look through magazines at the library. That way you'll know exactly what you're giving, and Mom and Dad will approve!)

- Send a check for them to spend however they desire—that always produces smiles. (Hint: sending cash through the mail is not a good idea.)

- Order a grandchild's gift online or through a mail-order catalog. You can even have your grandchildren mark several gift items they'd like. Then on their birthdays, you get to surprise them with your choice. Take advantage of direct shipping.

- Select age-appropriate gifts.

- Start your grandchild on a collection they are interested in.

- Give a gift of yourself—write a story, paint a picture, or share your craft.

Cousins as Far as the Eye Can See
Family Reunions

*Family faces are magic mirrors. Looking at people
who belong to us, we see the past, present and future.
We make discoveries about ourselves and them.*

—Gail Lumet Buckley

The Waltons of TV fame had three generations living together.
Today, families live miles apart and communicate through cyber-
space. How blessed we have been through technology! But family
reunions are sometimes impossible to attend. Here are tips if
branches of your family tree have to miss the big event:

- Take current photos of your missing family members to
  share with the reunion crowd. You can print photos at
  home or on a copier. Make enough so reunion attendees can
  have a copy to take home or forward them by e-mail. Be sure
  to include a brief update about their family happenings.

- Snap digital pictures of the reunion crowd to share with the
  missing family members.

- Videotape the entire reunion to share with missing family
  members.

- Choose one family member to make videotapes for all the
  reunion families.

- Appoint a cyber-savvy relative to create a family-reunion
  photo album. Using a digital camera, the entire photo collection can be sent in an instant.

- Connect with missing family branches by using the tiny Web camera on a laptop. Take a laptop and camera to the reunion, then have the missing family turn on their camera at the appointed time. Voilà! They can see and visit with the cousins!

Cool Classics
Books for a Summer Afternoon

A truly great book should be read in youth,
again in maturity and once more in old age, as a fine building
should be seen by morning light, at noon and by moonlight.

—ROBERTSON DAVIES

August afternoons are perfect for hiding out in a tent nestled under a shade tree and listening to a tape of Grandma and Grandpa reading some good storybooks. Instruct your grandkids on how to build a tent over the clothesline using old sheets and blankets. If there isn't a clothesline available, use a card table. Toss a blanket over it for a quick tent!

A popular online bookstore lists more than 101,000 children's books as classics. Take your pick and make an August videotape or cassette tape. The cassette tape is ideal for your grandchild to take outside and listen to. Here are a couple more book tips:

- Shop garage sales, library book sales, and used bookstores for bargain books.

- Send a copy of the books you read along with the tape or choose selections that are readily available at your grandchild's library. They will want to follow along.

Videos and DVDs

Videos and DVDs are a fun way to relax after a hard day of play. Bath time is over, pajamas are on—it's time to snuggle down for a good movie. You need to check with your son or daughter and see what type of viewing technology they are using. Almost everyone has a VCR, but many have moved on to the newest advance in technology, the DVD player. Once you know this vital information, you are ready to purchase some movies for the grandkids. Many of the book classics are available on VHS and DVD, so take your pick. (Suggestion: *Anne of Green Gables* by L. M. Montgomery is the perfect movie to lift your spirits. The scenery is beautiful, and the story is captivating.)

- Sandwich books with movies, then compare the book with the movies.

- Rent, or check out of the library, the movies you sent to grandkids. You watch them too. Then you can discuss them by phone, e-mail, or snail mail.

- Keep up with current movies and books. We've had wonderful writers in the past, and we have many talented writers today.

"Keep Cool" Care Package
Indoor Activities

Stay as cool as a cucumber!

—Gardener's slogan

August is the month when temperatures soar in most parts of the country. Send a "keep cool" care package to your grandchildren, including some of the following:

- Buy Popsicle molds and mail them along with some powdered drink mixes. Can't find Popsicle molds? Purchase small plastic cups and a bag of Popsicle sticks at your local craft store.

- Purchase a board game for your grandkids to play indoors when it's too hot to go outside. Monopoly and Scrabble are two good ones. Check with Mom and Dad on what they have. There are many new board games on the market.

- Begin a story on e-mail and have them add to it—send it back and forth until finished. You might write about their summer activities.

- Send a back-to-school gift certificate so your grandkids can go shopping in the cool of a store. They will love picking out a lunchbox, school supplies, or even a new outfit. The gift will soften the pangs of summer's end.

Growing Together
Blended Families

Blending doesn't just happen; we purposely journey into it.
—MAXINE MARSOLINI

Maxine Marsolini offers good advice for blending families in her books *Blended Families* (Moody, 2000) and *Blended*

Families Workbook (Pleasant Word, 2004). You may want to buy a copy for your blended family and for yourself. She encourages families to:

Become one family.

Listen with respect.

Encourage everyone equally.

Negotiate personal needs.

Deliver individual dreams.

These are good points for grandparents to remember too.

Connecting Spiritually
Write On!

My heart is overflowing with a beautiful thought!
I will write a lovely poem to the King, for I am as full of words
as the speediest writer pouring out his story.
—PSALM 45:1 TLB

When the grandchildren return to school and things slow down a bit for you, it's the perfect time to send a letter of encouragement to them. E-mail and letters are perfect for sharing a favorite verse of Scripture or one you have prayed for them. Start this practice when your grandchildren are young, and they will reciprocate by sharing verses with you too.

- Send a card or letter of encouragement to a grandchild through the postal service—all ages—toddlers to college. Everyone loves mail!

- Write a letter telling your grandchild how much he or she means to you. Praise, praise, praise!

- E-mail grandchildren if you don't have time to get a card in the mail—just write.

- Compliment them on their behavior during a recent visit.

Grand Tip of the Month
Connecting through the Written Word Transcends All Distance and Goes Straight to the Heart

Treasured letters between grandparents and grandchildren just keep on loving—once when first read, then every time they're read again.

—LD GRANDMA JANET TEITSORT

Keep a family letter document saved on your computer. This enables you to note the last grandchild that you wrote to and the news you sent, and it keeps the letter template handy. Just change the date, delete the old letter, and start fresh.

Recording the Legacy

Date_____

Long-distance activity/project _____

_____

Here's what my grandkids said_____

_____

Date_____

Long-distance activity/project _____

_____

Here's what my grandkids said_____

_____

Date_____

Long-distance activity/project _____

_____

Here's what my grandkids said_____

_____

Notes

_____

_____

_____

_____

_____

_____

_____

_____

_____

_____

_____

_____

_____

_____

_____

_____

Every leaf speaks bliss to me, fluttering
from the autumn tree.
—EMILY BRONTË

september

Brisk mornings and cool evenings signal seasonal changes. When you have lived many years, the changing seasons are easy to spot. But grandchildren with busy schedules often miss these cues from nature. This is where Grandpa and Grandma's expertise is needed. Point out the signs in nature that alert us to seasonal changes. Try some of these tips:

- Videotape a nature walk. Your grandkids will love seeing your daily walking route.

- E-mail your grandkids and mention the changes that signal the approaching season. If they, or you, live in a climate where there is little seasonal change, discuss that fact.

- Make an audiotape sharing stories about the Septembers you experienced as a child.

Fall into Fun!
Fun with Leaves

"Come, little leaves," said the wind one day.
"Come o'er the meadow with me and play.

Put on your dresses of red and gold;
Summer is gone, and the days grow cold."

—THOMAS J. CRAWFORD, ADAPTED BY TERRY KLUYTMANS

Autumn leaves fall, and that spells fun! You can do all sorts of projects that will make memories. Leaf rubbings and leaf painting on sweatshirts are two fun projects that can easily be demonstrated on videotape or Web camera. This is one project you will want to do before the leaves get too dry.

leaf rubbings

You will need:

- *Plastic-covered workspace*
- *Leaves from different kinds of trees*
- *White copy paper*
- *Old crayons (peel the paper off)*
- *Blue watercolor*
- *Watercolor paintbrush*
- *½ cup water*
- *Paper towel*
- *Inexpensive photo frame*
- *Black or dark blue pen or felt-tip marker*

Do:

1. *Place a leaf facedown on your workspace.*

2. *Cover with a sheet of paper (hold in place with one hand).*

3. *Use an unwrapped crayon and rub over the paper. Voilà! You will have a leaf imprint in your selected color!*

4. *Add plenty of water to your blue watercolor.*

5. *Dip your brush into the watercolor, then do a quick in-and-out in the water cup.*

6. *Brush your picture with a watery-blue mix.*

7. *Let dry, and you have a beautiful watercolor wash.*

8. *Frame and enjoy, or give as a gift.*

9. *Print the Bible verse: "Never will I leave you; never will I forsake you" (Hebrews 13:5) on the picture and suggest they give it to an elderly friend or neighbor.*

painting sweatshirts

You will need:

- *Plastic-covered workspace*
- *Cream-color sweatshirt*
- *Fabric paint in fall colors*
- *Different kinds of leaves*
- *Aluminum pie pans*
- *Wax paper to line inside of shirt body and sleeves*
- *Pins to hold wax paper in place*
- *Fabric pen or permanent black felt marker*

Do:

1. *Pour one color of paint into each pie pan.*

2. *Dip leaf into the paint and press onto the sweatshirt—*

remove and toss. Continue until front of shirt and sleeves are covered. Let dry thoroughly, then do the back of shirt and sleeves.

3. Use a permanent marker or fabric marker to print the principle from Hebrews 13:5 ("God Never Leaves Me") on the front of the shirt. Measure down one hand's width from neckline.

4. Cool sweatshirts to wear on a brisk autumn day!

Autumn—a Beautiful Word!
Fall Activities

For man, autumn is a time of harvest, of gathering together.
For nature, it is a time of sowing, of scattering abroad.
—Edwin Way Teale

Most people refer to the third season of the year as *fall*. But *autumn* is such a beautiful word, I think we should at least introduce our grandchildren to this fanciful name for fall. Here are some great ideas for celebrating the arrival of autumn with your grandkids:

- Share stories via phone, e-mail, or by postal service about the leaf forts you made as a child.

- Invite grandchildren and family who live in a tropical climate for an autumn visit. They get to experience the seasonal changes, and maybe you'll get to play in the leaves with them!

- Schedule an extended family vacation in a retreat area where there is fall foliage.

- Snap a seasonal postcard photo of your home.

- Search online for seasonal science projects. Learn why leaves change colors, how seasons are determined, and about seasonal changes. Your grandkids will love learning when Grandma and Grandpa are researching online with them. Use Instant Messenger for zipping info back and forth.

Autumn Apples

- Take advantage of the Internet, searching and finding all about John Chapman. Better known as Johnny Appleseed, he was born September 26, 1774.

- Make a videotape of you stirring up some appealing apple recipes: apple pies, apple dumplings, apple turnovers, applesauce, apple cake, apple butter, fried apples, stewed apples, apple crisp, and baked apples. (Try baking them in the microwave— five minutes for one.)

- Demonstrate how to use an apple peeler or (if you can) hand-peel an apple in one strip. The grandkids will love seeing and hearing Grandma share her specialties.

- Mail copies of the recipes and an apple recognition chart along with your videotape. These charts can be found in recipe books, libraries, and in some supermarkets. They describe a type of apple and suggest the apple dishes that it is best suited for.

- Do an apple craft for the older grandchildren and include it on your videotape. Slice apples and dry them in your oven. Create apple wreaths and garlands, accenting with cinnamon sticks and country ribbon. (Easy directions can be found on the Internet.) Yum, they smell like apple pie!

- Cut an apple diagonally and let your grandchildren discover the surprise star that hides within. Your videotape will be jammed full of activities!

- Show them how to plant apple seeds in a Styrofoam cup. They'll watch you do it on tape, then Mom and Dad can help them do likewise. Talk about the life cycle of the apple: seed, plant, tree, blossom, and fruit. Discuss the seasons in relationship to the apple cycle.

- Share your apple stories on tape, by e-mail, or in a letter. Do you have an apple tree? Do they? Share the best thing about having fruit trees. Share the most unpleasant part—such as picking up fruit before you can mow the lawn.

- Encourage your adult children to take the grandkids to an apple orchard.

Connecting Spiritually
Labor Day—the Work Ethic

Six days you shall labor and do all your work,
but the seventh day is a Sabbath to the LORD your God.
—EXODUS 20:9–10

Labor Day is celebrated on the first Monday of September. Families often view this holiday as the last hurrah of summer. Many children do not realize that Labor Day is a day set aside to honor working Americans. Let your grandchildren know what God has to say about work.

- Write out Exodus 20:9–10 at the end of an e-mail or letter.

- Jot a note about the wisdom of resting from our work. Even children know about stress!

- Discuss ways to honor the Sabbath.

- Speculate on how resting on the Sabbath would improve our emotional and physical health. (Note: point out that *Sabbath* is an Old Testament word referring to the last day of the week. Since the Resurrection of Jesus was on the first day of the week, most Christians observe the day of rest on the Lord's Day, or Sunday as we call it.)

Telling Tales of School
National Grandparents Day

Education is what remains after one has forgotten what one has learned in school.
—ALBERT EINSTEIN

In 1979 President Jimmy Carter proclaimed the first Sunday following Labor Day as National Grandparents Day. Many schools recognize grandparents by inviting them to visit students' classrooms. Long-distance grandparents who can't physically be there can participate in other ways.

- Use the search engine on your Internet and type in *National Grandparents Day*. You'll discover Web sites listing

125

information and activities to help you celebrate with your grandchild.

- Prepare a videotape or letter telling about your school days. Your grandchildren can proudly share information about their grandparents with the rest of the class. They won't feel left out—but they will feel special.

- Get started by answering these questions, then add additional stories of your own.

  - How did *you* get to school? If you rode a bus, how long was your bus ride?

  - Did you take your lunch? If so, what kind of foods did you pack? What did your lunchbox look like?

  - How big was your school? Was it a rural or a city school?

  - What were your teachers like? Did you have a favorite?

  - What kind of desks did you have?

  - Share your favorite playground activities. What other school stories do you remember?

  - What kind of grades did you make?

  - Did you ever get into trouble? Do you dare tell about it?

  - What were the clothing styles like?

  - What were your favorite extracurricular activities?

  - Who were your friends? Tell some friendship stories.

  - Was peer pressure a problem in your day?

By now your memory video is probably on Rewind, reviewing scenes from yesteryear. Share everything you can remember. Invite your grandchildren to reciprocate by telling about their school days too.

Sweep into Good Reading!
September Book Selections

*Books are the treasured wealth of the world and
the fit inheritance of generations and nations.*
—HENRY DAVID THOREAU

Online bookstores are a long-distance grandparent's dream. You can order books and have them shipped directly to your grandchild. These bookstores provide wonderful descriptions and reviews, plus you can take a peek into some books. Choose from a vast selection of books on autumn leaves and apples. Here are a couple you may want to include:

The Fall of Freddie the Leaf by Leo Buscaglia, PhD (Slack) is a story about the cycle of life. This seasonal book is helpful in explaining the seasons of life.

Apples by Ann L. Burckhardt (Bridgestone Books) is an easy reader. This book has bright, colorful photographs of apples. The book discusses different kinds of apples, the parts of an apple, where and how apples grow, and it even touches on the history of this delectable fruit.

leaf books via long distance

If you and your grandchildren live in different areas of the country, you can have double the fun and double the learning. Not only will grandkids learn about the different leaves in their area, but they will also learn about your geographical region. Much of the information shared can be done online or over the phone. You will have to use the postal service to mail some supplies and leaf exchanges, but the expense should be minor.

You will need:

- *Three-ring binder*
- *Plastic sleeves to hold letter-size copy paper (available at office-supply stores)*
- *Glue sticks*
- *Pens*
- *Books and wax paper for pressing leaves*

Do:

1. *Gather leaves and place between wax paper sheets, then tuck inside a book to press. Leave overnight or longer.*

2. *Glue leaf onto white copy paper and label. List the kind of leaf, where it was found, and any pertinent information.*

3. *Insert leaf sheet in clear plastic sleeve and arrange in binder.*

4. *After you gather the leaves from your area, mail the binder to your grandchild. Include extra plastic sleeves so they can add the leaves they've collected. Grandpas like helping with this project too.*

Blessings in a Box
Packing a Healthcare Box for College Grandkids

*You know, Grandma, when you bought that ice pack
to go in my first-aid kit, I was sure that I'd never use it. I never thought
I would sprain my foot so bad that I'd have to eat my own words.*

—CAROL RICHARDSON, AGE 18

If you have a college-bound grandchild, give them the wisdom of those who have gone before them. Polly Berent has written a book that answers any and all questions that students, parents, or grandparents may have. *Getting Ready for College: Everything You Need to Know before You Go* (Random House) is a survival guide to enable students to avoid pitfalls.

Grandparents can help by packing a "healthcare box." Now, that spells love! Your healthcare box, along with Polly Berent's book, will tell your grandchild how much you care. They will appreciate your thoughtfulness even more as the contents are needed and used.

Here are items to include in your healthcare box:

- Digital thermometer

- Ace bandage for sprains

- Safety pins for when they lose the metal clips for the Ace bandage

- Ice gel packs for bruises and swelling (Most students have refrigerators, not freezers.) But these get good and cold on the shelf in the fridge.

- Heat gel packs (Generally there is a microwave close by to heat these. Remind your grandchild to read the directions. If the packages are heated too long, they explode.)

- Adhesive heat wraps (Wonderful invention!)

- Band-Aids of different sizes

- Antibiotic ointment, such as Neosporin

- Eye drops

- Contact-lens solution (if needed)

- Benadryl cream or gel for insect bites, poison ivy

- Insect repellent

- Antacid, such as Mylanta

- Antihistamine, such as Benadryl, for allergy relief

- Pain relievers, such as aspirin, Advil, or Tylenol

- Cold medicine, such as Robitussin, Sudafed, or Dimetapp

- Azo for mild bladder infection

- Pepto Bismol for nausea

- Vitamin C and zinc lozenges for sore throats. (Take extra vitamin C during cold seasons.)

- Daily vitamins

- B vitamins for jumpy nerves

- Extra toothbrushes (They should throw away their toothbrush after being sick.)

- Cans or packets of chicken noodle soup

- Soup mug

- Bottle of 7-Up (to be reserved for illness)

Grand Tip of the Month
May Your Autumn Be Filled with Golden Moments of Caring and Sharing!

Grandma and Grandpa's love is a verb—
it always includes an act of caring and sharing.
—LD GRANDMA JANET TEITSORT

Grandparents, mark your calendar and send a monthly packet to your college grandchild. Prepaid calling cards and devotional magazines are nice for staying in touch and for encouraging them in their spiritual walk. Include some candy or a gift certificate to a favorite restaurant.

Recording the Legacy

Date_____

Long-distance activity/project _____

_____

Here's what my grandkids said_____

_____

Date_____

Long-distance activity/project _____

_____

Here's what my grandkids said_____

_____

Date_____

Long-distance activity/project _____

_____

Here's what my grandkids said_____

_____

Notes

_____

_____

_____

_____

_____

_____

_____

Few things are more delightful than grandchildren fighting over your lap.
—DOUG LARSON

october

Jack Frost has completed his painting. Autumn is now gowned in her finest. Shades of crimson, butterscotch, and russet decorate the countryside. Roadside markets are well stocked with pumpkins, gourds, and potted chrysanthemums. Festivals and craft shows provide economical entertainment for families as everyone enjoys the last few days of autumn splendor.

The Discovery
Columbus Day

In fourteen hundred ninety-two, Columbus sailed the ocean blue.
—"IN 1492"

Columbus Day falls on the second Monday in October. Students learn about this holiday in school, but grandparents can help make the information stick by expanding the study. Type *Columbus Day* on your Web search engine. Numerous sites will appear that contain facts to share and activities to do with your grandchild. You can do as much or as little as you desire. In addition you might want to try these:

- Present your grandchildren with a globe. There are many neat ones on the market. You can order one online and have it shipped to your grandchild.

- Check and see if your grandchildren have a world atlas CD for their computer; if not, this would be a welcomed gift.

- Send a box of Berry Blue Jell-O, clear plastic punch cups, and miniature ships or boats (purchase in a party shop). Ask Mom, Dad, or older grandchildren to help create this ocean snack by letting the Jell-O set in the punch cups. Add whipped topping, making "cool" waves, then set the miniature ships or boats on top. The little ones will love this surprise from Grandma and Grandpa!

The Frost Is on the Punkin
Ideas for the Pumpkin Patch

When the frost is on the punkin and the fodder's in the shock . . .
—JAMES WHITCOMB RILEY

By now the pumpkin seeds you sent to your grandchildren last spring have produced a plentiful pumpkin patch. If not . . .

- Send some money and persuade Mom and Dad to take the grandkids to a pumpkin patch, allowing each grandchild to pick out a pumpkin, compliments of Grandma and Grandpa. Be sure they videotape the outing!

- Tell your grandkids to measure around the pumpkins using

a measuring tape. Have them record the measurements. Ask if they think the size of the pumpkin has anything to do with the number of seeds inside.

- Make a videotape demonstrating all the pumpkin activities that can be done using pumpkins.

- Have Mom or Dad help them cut off the top of each pumpkin, scoop out the insides, and help them count the seeds.

- Wash the seeds, pat them dry, sprinkle with salt, and place them on a cookie sheet that has been sprayed with Pam.

- Bake the dried, salted seeds at 325 degrees for twenty to thirty minutes until crispy. They'll enjoy this healthy snack, and you will too!

Delicious Pumpkin Pie!
How to Cook a Pumpkin

But see, in our open clearings, how golden the melons lie;
enrich them with sweets and spices, and give us the pumpkin-pie!
—MARGARET JUNKIN PRESTON

Send your children a videotape with instructions on how to cook a pumpkin. Our busy lifestyles make canned pumpkin more practical for our baking needs, but whipping up recipes from a real pumpkin is a fun learning experience. First, select your pumpkin, wash the outside thoroughly, cut off the top, and scoop out the pulp and seeds. Next, you will need to choose how you want to cook your pumpkin. Today's modern conveniences provide numerous ways. Take your pick:

1. *Oven Baking:* Set the pumpkin without the lid in a pan of

water in the oven. Bake it until the sides of the pumpkin are tender (one hour at 325 degrees).

2. *Slow Cooker:* Cut up pumpkin shell, place in the Crock-Pot with a little bit of water, and cook on low until tender.

3. *Microwave:* Cut up your pumpkin shell and place in a microwave-safe dish with ½ cup of water. Cover with plastic wrap and cook until tender. Check every ten minutes until cooked. Cooking time will vary, but it will probably take about twenty minutes. (Watch the steam when removing the plastic wrap. Don't get burned! Tell the grandkids to let Mom or Dad do it.)

4. *Stovetop:* Cut up your pumpkin shell and boil in a pan on top of the stove until tender. This method requires a lot of watching; you don't want to let it boil dry.

What's Next?

- Mash your cooked pumpkin with a potato masher or mixer, then run it through a strainer.

- Get out your favorite recipe book and follow the recipe for a pumpkin pie.

- Explore recipes for pumpkin breads, rolls, or cookies. Delicious!

Who's Behind That Mask?
Halloween and Harvest Events

Whether it is a Halloween or a harvest party, your grandchildren will probably want to dress up in a costume. Here are some tips on celebrating this holiday long distance:

- Encourage your grandkids to dress up as storybook or biblical characters, candy (M&M, Hershey Kiss), cereal boxes, or appliances.

- Have Mom and Dad snap some photos with the digital camera and e-mail the pictures to you. If they use a regular camera, have them request double prints and send you a set. (Send some money to cover the additional cost!)

- Use your search engine and type in *Halloween*. Numerous Web sites will be listed, giving you lots of crafts, recipes, and interesting information.

- Research where Halloween originated and how it came to be celebrated in America.

- Tell them what the holiday was like when you were a child.

Connecting Spiritually
God's Word on Halloween

Whatever you do, whether in word or deed, do it all in the name of the Lord Jesus, giving thanks to God the Father through him.
—COLOSSIANS 3:17

Share what the Bible teaches about the occult (Deuteronomy 18:9–14). The world treats psychic readings, séances, Ouija boards, and horoscopes as if they are innocent and amusing activities. But what does God's Word say? Here's an opportunity to guide your grandkids to the Scriptures and let them discover the answers to their questions:

- Discuss via e-mail, letters, or phone the negative and positive sides of celebrating the holiday today. Have your grandkids consider if a harvest party will be a good alternative to celebrating Halloween.

- Make it a family decision. You and your extended families may not agree, but respect each other's decision. Some families opt to celebrate Halloween, ignoring those who want to turn the holiday into something evil. Others choose not to celebrate Halloween, deciding instead to have a harvest celebration for fun and fellowship. Together, decide your family's stand regarding this holiday.

Spiders, Owls, and Bats—Oh, My!
October Books and Crafts

October is crisp days and cool nights, a time to curl up around the dancing flames and sink into a good book.

—JOHN SINOR

Spiders, owls, bats, and things that go bump in the night tend to occupy the interests of many youngsters during October. Instead of fighting these interests, why not guide them? Here are a few great October books:

Stellaluna by Janell Cannon (Scholastic) is a children's book about a baby bat that gets separated from her mother. Research different kinds of bats using the Internet.

Owl Babies by Martin Waddell and illustrated by Patrick Benson (Candlewick Press) is the perfect book for children who experience insecurity when Mom leaves them in another's care. Send a package containing supplies so the grandchildren can create a picture of the owl babies. Make a sample picture and send the following directions.

directions for making an owl picture

You will need:

- *Black construction paper*
- *Glue sticks*
- *Stick pretzels*
- *Cotton balls*

Do:

1. Lay the pretzels on the black paper, forming tree branches.

2. Glue down the pretzels and let them dry.

3. Place two cotton balls, one above the other, on a pretzel branch and glue. The bottom cotton ball is for the body of the owl, and the top one is for the head.

4. Cut eyes and a beak from black construction paper and place them on the top cotton ball. Your grandkids will love snacking on the extra pretzels as they pursue this artistic endeavor.

The Itsy, Bitsy Spider by Iza Trapani (G. Stevens). Check your library and bookstore for more spider books.

Charlotte's Web by E. B. White (HarperCollins) is always fun to read again or watch the video instead. We all love Charlotte!

- Do some research on spiders and share via e-mail.

- Start a story web (see following directions) and mail on October 1. Set some ground rules—no murders, blood, or gore—just spooky! You may have to explain that *spooky* is when things seem to be frightening, but in the end, one discovers a logical explanation for the occurrence.

directions for making a story web

You will need:

- *Black yarn*
- *Black chenille sticks*
- *Plastic spider*

Do:

1. *Twist three black chenille sticks together at their centers. Spread them apart in a circular fashion. The six chenille arms will form the skeleton of the web.*

2. *Tie a piece of black yarn (two yards long) at the center of the sticks and secure with a knot.*

3. *Wrap the yarn loosely over and around each stick. Do not pull tightly or your circle will fold up. Each time you go around the circle, move the string outward an inch, then continue wrapping.*

4. *Begin telling your tale on tape or by letter.*

5. *Mail the spider web and your story to your oldest grandchild (use a 9 x 12 mailing envelope). If you have to fold the web together, send a picture of what it looks like opened. They'll catch on to what you are trying to do.*

6. *Have your grandchild add to the story and the web, then mail it back to you.*

7. *Finish the story and the web. Knot the yarn around the last chenille stick and add the plastic spider. Leave the extra yarn so they can hang the web in their room.*

8. *Mail the finished story web back to your grandchild—hopefully by the end of October.*

Patriotism—Grandparents' Style
Supporting Our Military Grandkids

He that would make his own liberty secure must guard even his enemy from oppression; for if he violates this duty he establishes a precedent that will reach himself.

—THOMAS PAINE

Having a grandchild in the military, either at home or abroad, produces all kinds of emotions within us. On the one hand, we are proud; but on the other, we have deep concerns for their welfare. Each day we place them in God's care and endeavor to make life easier for them and their family. Here are some things to do:

• Go to your favorite Web search engine and type *military families.* You'll be amazed at all the Web sites offering support and encouragement.

• Go to online bookstores and search for books for military families. Again, you'll be surprised at all the helpful resources. These make great gifts for your military family.

- Prepare a "talking" photo album (with your recorded voice) to be given as a Christmas gift for your military grandchild. These can be purchased online or at various stores. These albums contain enough pages for each member of the extended family to record a message and include a photo. Begin to snap those pictures now so you can send this gift early. What a welcomed gift for a deployed military grandchild!

Lullaby and Good Night
Bedtime Surprises

There never was a child so lovely
but his mother was glad to get him asleep.

—RALPH WALDO EMERSON

By now the nights are cool, and school is well in progress. Here are some suggestions for helping parents get their children to bed at a decent time:

- Send a short bedtime video. State that the video may only be watched after everyone is ready for bed. Invite them to sip apple juice and eat pretzels as they view the bedtime movie selection (with Mom's approval, of course!). You can mail funds for the treats.

- Plan a phone call to your grandchildren. Most homes have more than one phone, so you could have a conference call with two or three grandchildren in the same family.

- Make an appointment to visit with your grandchildren via Web camera before they go to bed.

- Mail a cassette tape to your grandchildren and ask them to record themselves reading from their school book after they are ready for bed. Mom mails the tape back to you. If they do this on a regular basis throughout the year, you will be able to keep abreast of their progress, praising and encouraging them.

- Mail new mugs for bedtime drinks. The drinks may be enjoyed while your grandchildren are listening to their sleepy-time tapes. But check with Mom first to make sure the kids are allowed to have drinks before bedtime!

- Send new pajamas—that always makes them want to get ready for bed. Practical gifts of sheets, blankets, and towel sets are available with character designs. (Check with Mom and Dad to find out the kids' favorite characters.) They'll love these extra-special touches and will drift off to dreamland thinking about Grandpa and Grandma.

Grand Tip of the Month
Begin and End Your Day by Connecting with Your Grandchild through Prayer and Activity

If I would have known that grandchildren were going to be so much fun I would have had them first!
—BILL LAURIN

Send your grandchildren a "talking" photo frame containing Grandma and Grandpa's picture. You can tell them good night and that you love them. They can play this recording every night. This is bound to make bedtime sweet!

Recording the Legacy

Date_____

Long-distance activity/project _____

_____

Here's what my grandkids said_____

_____

Date_____

Long-distance activity/project _____

_____

Here's what my grandkids said_____

_____

Date_____

Long-distance activity/project _____

_____

Here's what my grandkids said_____

_____

Notes

_____

_____

_____

_____

_____

_____

_____

november

According to the calendar, it is still autumn. But if you live in an area of seasonal changes, late fall often brings winterlike weather. Outside, broomstick trees stretch branches heavenward, making silhouettes against the sky. Squirrels scamper to and fro, stockpiling food for winter. November has arrived.

Squirrel Spying
Watching Our Furry Friends

To every thing there is a season,
and a time to every purpose under the heaven.
—ECCLESIASTES 3:1 KJV

Do your grandchildren have a squirrel in their yard? Do you have one in yours? Here's an opportunity for learning and sharing:

- Correspond via e-mail, letter, or phone about the squirrel(s) in both of your yards.
- Use the digital camera and e-mail photos of your squirrel(s).

- Write a story about your squirrel(s) and have them write about theirs. Be sure to illustrate your stories.

- Research on the Internet about the many different types of squirrels.

- Check at the library and bookstores for some nature books on squirrels, and of course, some storybooks! Beatrix Potter watched animals as a child. Out of that came her classics: *The Tale of Squirrel Nutkin, The Tale of Peter Rabbit,* and many others. Who knows, you may be nurturing a budding author!

Our Hearts Gather Together
Thanksgiving

Forever on Thanksgiving Day, the heart will find the pathway home.
—WILBUR D. NESBIT

Thanksgiving will soon arrive, so think about celebrating this season of thankfulness all month long. If your family is not able to get together for the holiday, there are many ways to establish Thanksgiving traditions across the miles. Try some of these ideas:

- Start a thanksgiving letter. Mail it from family to family, asking each one to write about the past year and the things they are thankful for.

- Read the letter aloud on Thanksgiving Day. Not possible? Then fax or mail everyone a copy. Save the letters from year to year and place them in a family scrapbook.

- Tune into each other via the Web camera.

- Share a phone call.

- Videotape your family dinners and mail each other copies.

- Exchange recipes for traditional dishes such as noodles or sweet potato casserole. There's comfort in knowing that even though families may be separated by miles, they are eating the family's favorite recipes.

Pilgrim Play
The First Thanksgiving

Enter his gates with thanksgiving and his courts with praise;
give thanks to him and praise his name.
—PSALM 100:4

Involve older grandchildren by having them research the first Thanksgiving on the Internet or at the library. Then have them help you make the story of the first Thanksgiving come alive with meaning for the younger grandkids. The older grandkids will enjoy helping you plan some creative play, such as these great ideas:

- Create or purchase some dress-up clothes (pilgrim and Native American costumes) and have the grandkids act out the first Thanksgiving. Ages four to eight especially love the playacting.

- Read and mail a book that tells about the pilgrims' first voyage. If the grandchildren are coming to visit or if you're traveling to them, you can be in on the fun. If you can't be together, read the book to them on tape or video.

Sailing on the Mayflower

Acting out a story is a wonderful way to remember facts. Get someone to videotape the entire drama. Make a memory!

- Line up kitchen chairs or use the space between two twin beds to represent the ship. (Choose any narrow space that will recreate the cramped quarters on the ship.)

- Give each child a shoebox or small suitcase with one change of clothes, a Bible, and one toy. That is all the pilgrims could take with them.

- Pack each child a meal of cold biscuit (the pilgrims called it hardtack) and dried beef (salted meat).

- Have the children stay on board for thirty minutes—or a length of time that seems like a long time for the little ones.

- Discuss what it would be like to stay on the ship for many weeks.

Popcorn Activities

Thanksgiving is also a time to celebrate the bountiful fall harvest, and what cornucopia would be complete without corn on the cob? Celebrate the harvest season with the next best thing—popcorn!

- Mail some (microwave) packets of different flavored popcorn to the grandkids.

- Encourage them to try the popcorn with milk and sugar, eating it like cereal. (The pilgrims and early settlers ate popcorn this way.) The brave and daring will discover that it's quite tasty!

- String popcorn (send string and needles for this purpose) and place the garlands outside on tree branches for the birds to eat. The grandkids can also string popcorn and save the garland for the Christmas tree—if Mom says it's OK.

- Have the grandkids fix popcorn (with Mom and Dad's help) in different ways: microwave and air popper.

- Have Dad pour a little oil in a covered pan and pop some corn on the stove. Show them a picture of an old-fashioned corn popper.

- Purchase microwave popcorn that is still on the cob. Butter the corn and place the cob in the microwave bag that comes with it. Follow the directions for cooking time. Popcorn does grow on a cob! (You may find this corn in the gourmet food section.)

A Bountiful Harvest
Books and Movies

Books are not made for furniture, but there is nothing else that so beautifully furnishes a house.
—Henry Ward Beecher

The Foxfire series (Anchor Press/Doubleday) is great for older grandchildren. The books in this series describe the pioneer life of people living in the Appalachian region.

Thanksgiving Is Here! by Diane Goode (Harper Collins), is a good book choice for this month's taped reading. This book will make you smile!

The Very First Thanksgiving Day by Rhonda Gowler Greene, illustrated by Susan Gaber (Atheneum), is a beautiful book that will transport children back to the first thanksgiving.

Check online bookstores for other books on cornhusk dolls. When you send the book, also send supplies and directions on how to make a cornhusk doll.

Samuel Eaton's Day by Kate Waters, photos by Russ Kendall (Scholastic), and **Sarah Morton's Day** by Kate Waters, photos by Russ Kendall (Scholastic), are beautifully done. They will help your grandchild visualize the life of the early settlers.

Squanto: A Warrior's Tale, starring Adam Beach, is an excellent movie. If you can't find it in the stores, it can be ordered at an online bookstore. Videos and books on Squanto's life will help the children understand more about this period in history. There are many versions available.

Flexible Grandparents
Blended Families and Holidays

If it is possible, as far as it depends on you,
live at peace with everyone.

—ROMANS 12:18

Tying the Family Knot by Terri Clark (Broadman & Holman) is a must-read for every adult member of a blended family. Here is a list of "do be's" that will help tie your family together.

- Do be sensitive to the feelings of all grandchildren—bonus and biological. Whatever you do for one, do for the other.

- Do be flexible and willing to change celebration times to accommodate visitation schedules.

- Do be interested in the lives of all your grandchildren.

Converse with each one, talking about the things that are important to them.

- Do be organized. Write birthdays and important events of all grandchildren on the calendar.

- Do be open to accepting and starting new holiday traditions. Perhaps something as simple as making a new family member's favorite holiday dish will help tie your family knot. Maybe the bonus grandkids like a certain kind of cookie that you've never made. They'll love it if you'll make them some!

- Do be gracious and kind, accepting the blessings of your blended family—for that's what they are—a double blessing!

Connecting Spiritually
Touching Hearts with Thankfulness

But the fruit of the Spirit is love, joy, peace, patience, kindness, goodness, faithfulness, gentleness and self-control.

—GALATIANS 5:22–23

The celebration of Thanksgiving provides the perfect opportunity for you to introduce some spiritual teachings from the Bible.

cornucopia and the fruit of the spirit

You will need:

- *Plastic fruit (nine pieces)*

- *Roll of tape*
- *Paper tags*

Do:

1. *Mail a cornucopia to each household of your grown children.*

2. *Write out Galatians 5:22–23 and the following directions: Read the Scripture and label each of the plastic fruits with one of the fruits of the Spirit. Use the filled cornucopia as a Thanksgiving decoration.*

3. *Write a letter reminding your children and grandchildren that in order to have a harvest, the seed has to be planted, cultivated, and nourished. Point out that the fruit of the Spirit is the harvest from a Spirit-controlled life.*

4. *Encourage them to plant spiritual seeds by inviting the Holy Spirit into their hearts and being filled with the Spirit through prayer and Bible reading.*

Sharing Thanksgiving Scriptures

- Search the Psalms each day and e-mail thanksgiving scriptures to your grandchildren. Invite your grandchildren to do likewise.

- Research the Festival of Tabernacles (or Ingathering), celebrated by the Israelites as a thanksgiving for the harvest.

Prayer Boxes

- Give each grandchild a prayer box (any small box will do). The purpose of the box is to hold the praise listings or prayer requests of your grandchildren. Make sure they understand and respect the fact that a prayer box is private—like a diary.

- Include a bag of colored stones. Tell the grandkids that the stones are to be used with their prayers. The stones may represent the requests or problems they are giving to the Lord. As they place the stones in the box, tell them to visualize giving their problems to the Lord.

- End the season of thanksgiving with this tasty activity. German monks made the first pretzels as a reward for children who learned to say their prayers. The pretzel shape represents the crossed arms of children at prayer. Share this bit of information with your grandchildren and mail them several different kinds of pretzels. Wrap them in bubble wrap so they won't break.

pretzels

- *Waxed paper*
- *1 bag frozen bread dough, or 1 can breadstick dough*
- *Beaten egg white*
- *Salt*

Give each child a small portion of dough and a piece of waxed paper. Roll the dough (using the palm of their hand) on the wax paper to form a long roll. Twist the dough into a pretzel shape, representing praying hands. Have Mom brush the pretzels with beaten egg white and sprinkle with salt. Bake until golden brown (about ten minutes).

- Order pretzels online and have them shipped to your grandkids.

- Search online for sites about pretzels. There are numerous ones worth visiting.

- Videotape yourself making some pretzels; send a container of your baked pretzels, along with the directions.

Share a Hobby
Pass On a Skill

In this age of long-distant grandparenting, you don't have to be thankful that you're apart. But choose to be thankful that you can connect through modern technology. The pioneers weren't as fortunate.

—LD Grandma Janet Teitsort

Blessed are the grandparents who take the time to hand down a skill or craft to their grandchildren. It may be as simple as making lemonade from real lemons or stitching quilt squares together. In each family the skills are different, but the blessing is the same—a special bonding between the grandparent and the grandchild. When your grandchildren visit, introduce the craft or skill, then provide them with materials to continue at home. You can share a love for:

- Sewing
- Knitting or crocheting
- Reading or writing
- Art
- Pottery
- Cooking
- Planting
- Nature—birds, foliage, fishing, etc.
- Woodcrafts
- Farming
- Animals
- Golf

- Collections
- Sports
- Music

The possibilities are as limitless as your interests. Remember, whatever your hobby, your grandchildren may share the same interests, for there is a little bit of you in each grandchild.

Spin a Yarn
Sharing Your Life Story

Our stories are inextricably interwoven. What you do is part of my story; what I do is part of yours.
—Daniel Taylor

Every life is unique, and that means yours! Grandchildren love to hear about the "good old days." Take the time to share the stories that won't be told unless you tell them. Share the stories that only you know! Since the grandkids are busy, and you are too, there is seldom time to sit around and have leisurely conversations. Besides that, there are miles between you, and your stories may be a little much to share by phone or e-mail. But you can still pass on your stories.

- Write a "personal journal of remembering" for your grandchild. Make copies for all the grandkids. Be sure to take a look at the parent and grandparent journals available in the bookstores. These journals ask key questions to jog our memories. By tackling one question a day, you'll soon have a lasting legacy for your grandchild.

- Record on cassette tape stories about your life. If you don't like to write, you still might want to invest in one of the journaling books on the market. These books cover every possible event of a life and will give you ideas for sharing on tape.

- Make a videotape of you sharing life stories. That will be even better!

Grand Tip of the Month
Unite with Thankful Hearts!

Gratitude greatly improves attitude; big and little folks alike!
—LD GRANDMA JANET TEITSORT

Keep a gratitude journal and encourage your grandchildren to do likewise. Each night write at least three things that you are thankful for. The items can be things that have occurred during the day or blessings you recognize, such as your health.

Recording the Legacy

Date_____

Long-distance activity/project _____

_____

Here's what my grandkids said_____

_____

Date_____

Long-distance activity/project _____

_____

Here's what my grandkids said_____

_____

Date_____

Long-distance activity/project _____

_____

Here's what my grandkids said_____

_____

Notes

_____

_____

_____

_____

_____

_____

_____

_____

_____

_____

_____

_____

_____

_____

_____

_____

_____

_____

_____

_____

_____

_____

At Christmas play and make good cheer,
for Christmas comes but once a year.
—THOMAS TUSSER

december

The Christmas season has arrived! It's time to plan how you will celebrate the holidays with your long-distance family. There are places to go, cookies to bake, things to buy, and packages to wrap. There's no time to waste, so let's get busy!

Shopping Made Easy!
Gift Buying

Christmas is for children. But it is for grownups too. Even if it is a headache, a chore, and nightmare, it is a period of necessary defrosting of chill and hide-bound hearts.

—LENORA MATTINGLY WEBER

Hopefully, you have been shopping all year with this month in mind. Planning is the name of the game. You don't want to be in a last-minute frenzy! Packages need to be mailed the first week or two of December in order to arrive on time. Here are some tips on gift storage:

- Keep a running list of purchases for your family on your

home computer. Save it in your computer and print a copy to carry in your purse. Use two columns: one for birthdays and one for Christmas.

- Keep gifts in plastic storage tubs throughout the year. Be sure you store them in a dry place. Note the location of storage on your list of gifts.

Catalog or Online Orders

- Let your grandchildren look through catalogs and mark the items they like. If both of you have the same catalog, items may be marked during a phone conversation or via e-mail. Your grandchildren can give you the page numbers, guiding you to their selections.

- Surprise your grandkids by picking one or more of the gifts. Be sure they understand that you are not buying all the things they mark. You don't want to set them up for disappointment, nor do you want them to become greedy.

- Check with Mom before ordering so you don't duplicate items.

- Have the catalog company ship the gift(s) to your grandchild's home. Some companies will even gift wrap the items. You don't have to bother with the wrapping or mailing!

- If you are Internet savvy, many online toy stores feature a Wish List option, in which the grandchildren can select the items they want. Once each grandchild's wish list is created (by the grandchild or parent), you can view the list online and make your purchases. Most Web stores will also give you the option of having the present wrapped and shipped directly to your grandchild's home.

Gift Ideas Galore

- Think smaller gifts. The increased cost of postage and frustration of packaging may make you want to consider giving gift cards to major stores.

- Send a check to Mom or Dad and have them shop for the grandkids. The upside of this is the grandkids will receive just what they wanted from you. The downside is you don't feel very involved.

- Give a family keepsake. Do you have a family heirloom you want to give to a certain grandchild? Christmas may be the time to do it!

- Include an inexpensive, wrapped item when you give a gift check, gift card, or savings bond to your grandkids. Everyone likes receiving money, but it's nice to have something to unwrap too.

- Make a craft. Have Grandpa build a dollhouse and partially furnish it. Continue furnishing it with miniatures each Christmas. This also works with railroads or racetracks. You can keep adding miniatures through the years.

- Start the grandkids on collectibles. (Be sure that you choose something they are interested in.) Music boxes, teddy bears, dolls, trains, and cars are just a few ideas.

- Choose a gift that keeps on giving—give a magazine subscription! (Check with Mom and Dad to find out appropriate magazines the kids are reading.)

- Shop, package, and mail it all if you're up to it. But remember to have your Christmas packages in the mail the first or second week of December. Then sit back and enjoy the rest of the month.

'Tis the Season to Be Jolly
Decorating Away the Long-Distance Blues

This is the message of Christmas: we are never alone.
—TAYLOR CALDWELL

If the extended family can't come home for Christmas, you can hang in there by hanging the grandkids' pictures on the Christmas tree. Here are some ideas:

- Buy wallet-size picture frames to fit your décor, attach ribbons or bows, and space the pictures around your tree. Also, talking photo Christmas ornaments are available. Type in *talking photo ornaments* in your Web search engine to make your selection. Presto! You have the entire family home for Christmas. You'll enjoy seeing your smiling cherubs each time you walk by the tree, and what a conversational piece it will be!

- Ask your adult children to trace the grandkids' hand prints and mail them to you. Then cut them out of two or three contrasting fabrics, decorate with bits of lace and ribbon, and hang the fabric handprints on your tree. You have a wonderful homemade ornament that reminds you of your special little ones.

- Send hometown Christmas to your son or daughter's family by passing on some ornaments from years gone by, providing a written description of their significance to the grandkids. There is comfort in knowing that objects from each home are intermingled.

- Snap photos of your household decorations, inside and out. Have your son or daughter do the same, then exchange photos by e-mail or snail mail.

- Discuss and share Christmas traditions and recipes by phone, e-mail, or by letters. Pass down those cookie recipes that spell Christmas for your family!

- Order double prints of all Christmas photos taken in each household. Share these with each other. If the extended family can't be together, then share the memories in photos.

- Start new traditions, such as:

  - Phone calls at appointed times on the holidays

  - Reading the Christmas story from the Bible via Web camera or by speakerphone

  - Each extended family bakes a birthday cake for Baby Jesus

  - Start an "I remember one Christmas . . ." letter. Write a special memory and mail it to another family member, who adds their story. That family member in turn mails it on to the next in line, and so on. This can be done via e-mail or by regular mail. Make copies of the completed letter and send everyone a copy!

Home for the Holidays
Grandparents of College Students
At Christmas, all roads lead home.
—MARJORIE HOLMES

Finals

Final-exams' week (usually the second week in December) is a great time to let your college grandkids know how much you love and appreciate them. Try the following ideas:

- Send a care package of nutritious snacks and foods for the week of final exams.

- Say lots of prayers for your grandchild. Pray for them to use wisdom in getting sleep, eating healthy, and studying. Pray for their minds to be keen and alert.

Home, but Still Long Distance

College kids are always short on funds, so brighten up their holiday break by treating them to a "just because I love you" gift. The following list of gifts is not meant to take the place of their Christmas gift from you, but any selection would be an added treat.

- Share lots of phone calls and use the Web camera.

- Mail a new-release video or DVD and some snacks. They can invite their friends over for a movie.

- Treat them to tickets at a movie theater or gift certificates for a video store.

- Give them gift certificates for their favorite restaurant.

• Bless them with some extra cash for gift buying and gas for visiting friends.

Visions of Books Danced in Their Heads
Christmas Books to Delight

Do give books—religious or otherwise—for Christmas.
They're never fattening, seldom sinful, and permanently personal.
—LENORE HERSHEY

Books are always special, but Christmas stories seem to touch the hearts of young and old alike! Make an audio or videotape of you and Grandpa reading some Christmas books. The grandkids will love hearing your voices and seeing you. Don't forget, you can always read a story or two on a Web camera. It's the next best thing to being there.

Rudolph the Red-Nosed Reindeer (several versions available) will be enjoyed in book, song, or movie format. Add an inflatable plastic reindeer when you mail this much-loved story. You're bound to hear squeals of delight when you talk to the grandkids on the phone!

The Night Before Christmas by Clement Moore is a classic that you will want to purchase for your grandkids. Mailing a toy Santa along with the book will thrill your little ones!

The Polar Express by Chris Van Allsburg (Houghton Mifflin) is a beautiful book about a boy's train ride to the North Pole, where Santa gives the boy a bell from a reindeer's harness. If your grandchild is old enough, a bell on a satin ribbon makes a nice accompaniment for this book and tape. A small wooden train set could also add hours of imaginative play.

The Giant Hug by Sandra Horning and illustrated by Valerie Gorbachev (Knopf Books for Young Readers) is not a Christmas book, but it is a perfect "anytime" book for long-distance families. It would make an excellent Christmas gift. The story is about Owen the pig who is determined to send his grandmother a giant hug for her birthday. Read a copy of this book via video or use a Web cam. Then mail them a copy to keep, and be sure to send bags of Hersey's Hugs and Kisses chocolate candies with it.

Alabaster's Song by Max Lucado and illustrated by Michael Garland (Tommy Nelson) is a Christmas story about a boy and the angel atop the Christmas tree. This wonderful story is also available on video or DVD.

The Crippled Lamb by Max Lucado and his daughters, Jenna, Andrea, and Sara (Tommy Nelson), is another winning story. The beautiful illustrations are by Liz Bonham. This is truly a precious story that melts hearts, and it is also available on video or DVD.

The Jolly Christmas Postman by Allan and Janet Ahlberg (Scholastic) is unique. Since long-distance grandparents and grandchildren are familiar with the postal service, this is a must-have. The book is filled with envelopes containing delightful surprises.

Children around the World Celebrate Christmas by Susan T. Osborn and Christine Tangvald (Standard) will add a touch of culture. The beautiful illustrations are by Jodie McCallum. Collect "Christmas around the World" ornaments to share with your grandchild. Share recipes of Christmas cookies and pastries that originated in other countries. Make learning fun!

The Candymaker's Gift: A Legend of the Candy Cane by Helen and David Haidle (Chariot Victor) tells the story of a candy maker who made the first candy cane, explaining what the candy represents.

Remember to visit your local and online bookstores and browse, browse, browse through the children's Christmas book sections. There are always new releases among the "golden oldies" that have become classics to treasure. You're bound to pick the perfect book for you and your grandchild to share!

Homemade Christmas
Christmas Crafts
Something about an old-fashioned Christmas is hard to forget.
—HUGH DOWNS

Christmas wouldn't be Christmas if Grandma and the grandchildren didn't do a few crafts. After all, homemade is straight from the heart! Use your favorite online search engine and type in *Christmas crafts*. You'll discover wonderful sites with numerous ideas. But here are some projects that you will want to try too. They're guaranteed to provide some delightful hours of Christmas fun for you and the grandkids. If you're not going to be able to get together in person, you'll want to make a demonstration video, plus send some supplies for the projects.

graham cracker houses

You will need:

- *Empty pint carton (milk, whipping cream, or half-and-half)*
- *Powdered sugar*

- *Graham crackers*
- *Miniature marshmallows*
- *Gumdrops*
- *Licorice*
- *Candy canes*
- *Candy kisses*
- *Other favorite candies*

Do:

1. *Make a spreadable paste of powdered sugar and water.*

2. *Spread paste on all sides of the pint carton, and apply one rectangle of graham cracker to each side.*

3. *Break a graham cracker in half and apply the halves to the slanted top to make a roof.*

4. *Glue miniature marshmallows to the tip sides of the carton and let dry.*

5. *Fill in, using marshmallows, where the crackers meet on the sides.*

6. *Create doors and windows using the other candies.*

Fun, fun, fun! These graham-cracker houses are not to eat; they're just for looks—but you can enjoy the leftovers! Have the grandchildren spread some icing on the extra crackers and enjoy. Yum, yum, yum!

cinnamon ornaments

Not only do these ornaments make your house smell heavenly, but they can be given as gifts to schoolteachers, Sunday school teachers, neighbors, and shut-ins.

You will need:

- *4 ounces ground cinnamon*
- *¾ cup applesauce*
- *2 tablespoons white school glue*

Do:

1. Mix the ingredients thoroughly.

2. Roll out the dough.

3. Cut out shapes with cookie cutters.

4. Poke a hole in the top of the shape before it totally dries (use a drinking straw).

5. Allow the ornaments to dry thoroughly (this may take several hours).

homemade potpourri

If you want your house to be filled with the smells of an old-fashioned Christmas, make some potpourri. Several days before you begin this project, buy some oranges, eat them, and save the peels. You can invite your friends to help you eat the oranges or serve the family an orange salad. You'll find a way. Besides, think how healthy everyone will be consuming all that vitamin C!

You will need:

- *Dried orange peels*
- *Whole cloves*
- *Ground cinnamon*
- *Fresh pine needles gathered from trees*
- *Large bowl or pan for mixing*

- *Vinyl tablecloth*
- *Scissors*

Do:

1. *Spread the vinyl tablecloth over your workspace.*

2. *Snip the orange peels into small pieces, using scissors.*

3. *Remove the pine needles from the branches and cut into short pieces.*

4. *Mix the orange peels and pine needles.*

5. *Add the whole cloves.*

6. *Sprinkle the entire mixture with ground cinnamon.*

7. *Line small basket with foil (or use any container), add the mixture, and place throughout your home. The aroma is heavenly!*

potpourri hot pads

You will need:

- *Potpourri mixture*
- *Scissors*
- *Fabric cut to the size of a hot pad*
- *Quilt batting cut to the size of a hot pad (Hint: if you're mailing these supplies to your grandkids, precut the fabric squares and quilt batting.)*
- *Needle and thread*
- *Large ladle or spoon*

Do:

1. *Place two layers of fabric with right sides facing each other. (The wrong side should be facing you.)*

172

2. Layer with the quilt batting.

3. Spoon the potpourri mixture on top of the batting.

4. Cover with another layer of quilt batting.

5. Hand-stitch around the outside edge, leaving one side open.

6. Turn one layer back and over the quilt batting.

7. Stitch along the open seam, folding raw edges to the inside.

When you set a warm dish on this hot pad, it will fill your home with a "homemade Christmas" scent!

Connecting Spiritually
The Christmas Story

I truly believe that if we keep telling the Christmas story, singing the Christmas songs, and living the Christmas spirit, we can bring joy and happiness and peace to this world.

—NORMAN VINCENT PEALE

Christmas is a perfect time to connect spiritually with your extended family. Read and discuss the Christmas story with your little ones, helping them understand the significance of the birth of Jesus Christ, the son of God.

- Establish a spiritual tradition by having Grandpa or Grandma read the Christmas story on audio or videotape.

- Read the Christmas story via the Web camera. Have the entire extended family gather around for this blessed event.

- If you're using the Web camera, have the family take turns reading the story.

- Have each grandchild read a different section of the

173

Christmas story, then illustrate their scene. Assemble the pages into a family Christmas book.

Christmas Cheer All Year Long
Christmas Card Recycling

*I will honor Christmas in my heart,
and try to keep it all the year.*

—CHARLES DICKENS

There are lots of creative ways to recycle the beautiful Christmas cards we receive from friends and family each year. Try one of these project ideas:

miniature advent or gift boxes

Grandma, save your Christmas cards from year to year to form miniature Advent or gift boxes. These card boxes are great to send to your grandkids in place of an Advent calendar. Send one set of twenty-five boxes filled with Scripture and wrapped candies. This is a great way to spiritually connect with your family through the Christmas holiday.

The easy thing about this craft is you can do it while watching TV, and it's so much fun seeing these cute little boxes take shape! You can count on it: you'll have to teach the grandkids how to make them too!

You will need:

- *Scissors*
- *Whiteout*
- *Christmas cards*

Do:

1. *Cut apart the card on the fold and do the following steps on each card half. (The front of the card will be the top of your box, and the inside message will form the bottom of your box.)*

2. *Use the Liquid Paper to remove the name of the sender before recycling your cards.*

3. *Fold all the sides up one or two inches, depending on the size of the card. (Fold the top so the picture will show on the outside of your box. Fold the bottom so the message will be on the inside of your box.)*

4. *Snip in on one fold at each corner.*

5. *Fold up the sides, overlapping the flaps to form a box corner.*

6. *Staple or tape the corners of the box.*

Other Decorative Ways to Recycle Christmas Cards

- Delight your grandkids with a postcard cut from the front of a recycled Christmas card. Write a short note on the back and send through the mail! The winter scenes on the cards make these perfect for several months.

- Devise some homemade sewing cards. Cut off the front of last year's Christmas card and punch around all four sides of the card with a hole punch. Mail several of these to the grandkids with some yarn and plastic darning needles. They'll love this new and inexpensive craft!

- Design gift tags, using decorative scrapbooking scissors.

- Decorate inexpensive gift bags or even brown paper bags

with recycled card fronts. Edge them with scrapbooking scissors and add handles from jute.

- Dream up some new ornaments by cutting out the pictures and edging with beaded trim or ribbon.

- Donate card fronts to Saint Jude's Ranch for Children, 100 St. Jude Street, Boulder City, Nevada 89005. Get the entire extended family started on this worthwhile project. The children at St. Jude recycle the card fronts, package the recycled cards, and sell them to earn spending money. They use all types of greeting cards, not just Christmas cards. What better way to teach your grandchildren to reach out and help others in need!

Shepherd Bear

Shepherd Bear, from my Touching Hearts gift line, is a fun way for a family to share the Christmas story. The bear, dressed in a shepherd's costume, carries a shepherd's bag filled with memorabilia commemorating the first Christmas night. Scripture references are given, and the family may participate in the reading of the selected passages. Bears may be ordered directly through Touching Hearts, P.O. Box 129, Westport, IN 47283.

Grand Tip of the Month

This Christmas, May the Christ Child Be Born Anew in the Heart of Every Member of Your Extended Family!

And a little child will lead them.

—ISAIAH 11:6

Divide your Christmas gift list into twelve short lists. Each month shop for the names on your list. When December rolls around, you're almost finished!

Recording the Legacy

Date_____

Long-distance activity/project _____
_____

Here's what my grandkids said_____
_____

Date_____

Long-distance activity/project _____
_____

Here's what my grandkids said_____
_____

Date_____

Long-distance activity/project _____
_____

Here's what my grandkids said_____

Notes

_____
_____
_____
_____
_____
_____
_____
_____

sharing the legacy

As a long-distance grandma, you've undoubtedly had lots of fun making the miles melt away between you and your grandchildren as you shared the projects in this book with your beloved offspring.

My guess is that you also came up with a few ideas of your own. Now is the time to get those ideas down on paper so you can keep them handy for future use and, even more, so you can pass them on to generations to come. As a matter of fact, this entire book, with your handwritten notes, makes a wonderful keepsake to pass on to your children and grandchildren.

Use this and the following pages to record your own ideas for connecting with your grandchildren or to chronicle your thoughts about those special children who add so much joy to your life.

about the author

Janet Teitsort is the author of *Rainbows for Teachers, Treasures for Teachers, Seasons of Laughter for Teachers,* and *Quiet Times: Meditations for a Busy Woman.* Janet has contributed to *Proverbs for Busy Women* and *The Ultimate Bible Guide.* Her publishing credits include *Mature Living, Today's Christian Senior, Mature Years, Liguorian, The Secret Place, The Christian Reader,* and many others.

Janet is a graduate of CLASS (Christian Leaders, Authors, and Speakers Services) and enjoys public speaking. She and her husband, John, make their home in Westport, Indiana. They are the parents of two children and proud grandparents of nine grandchildren.